The BIG MINNESOTA REPRODUCIBLE Activity Book!

BY CAROLE MARSH

This activity book has material which correlates with Minnesota People and Cultures Framework.

At every opportunity, we have tried to relate information to the Minnesota History and Social Science, English, Science, Math, Civics, Economics, and Computer Technology directives.

For additional information, go to our websites:
www.theminnesotaexperience.com or **www.gallopade.com.**

Published by

GALL**O**PADE™
INTERNATIONAL

800-536-2GET
www.gallopade.com

Reading / Reference / Research / Reinforcement

Gallopade is proud to be a member or supporter of these educational organizations and associations:

NSSEA   ASCD   ABA AMERICAN BOOKSELLERS ASSOCIATION   APPL ASSOCIATION OF PARTNERS FOR PUBLIC LANDS SUPPORTER   NCSS

The Big Activity Book Team

Billie Walburn

Michael Marsh

Antoinette Miller

Michele Yother

Carole Marsh

Pam Dufresne

Steven Saint-Laurent

Bob Longmeyer

Kathy Zimmer

Chad Beard

Cranston Davenport

Shery Kearney

Sherry Moss

Cecil Anderson

Pat Newman

Jackie Clayton

Terry Briggs

Victoria DeJoy

Al Fortunatti

Published by

GALLOPADE™
INTERNATIONAL

800-536-2GET
www.gallopade.com

The Minnesota Experience Series

My First Pocket Guide to Minnesota!

The Minnesota Coloring Book!

My First Book About Minnesota!

Minnesota Jeopardy: Answers and Questions About Our State

Minnesota "Jography!": A Fun Run Through Our State

The Minnesota Experience! Sticker Pack

The Minnesota Experience! Poster/Map

Discover Minnesota CD-ROM

Minnesota "GEO" Bingo Game

Minnesota "HISTO" Bingo Game

A Word From The Author

Minnesota is a very special state. Almost everything about Minnesota is interesting and fun! It has a remarkable history that helped create the great nation of America. Minnesota enjoys an amazing geography of incredible beauty and fascination. The state's people are unique and have accomplished many great things.

This Activity Book is chock-full of activities to entice you to learn more about Minnesota. While completing puzzles, coloring activities, word codes, and other fun-to-do activities, you'll learn about your state's history, geography, people, places, animals, legends, and more.

Whether you're sitting in a classroom, stuck inside on a rainy day, or—better yet—sitting in the back seat of a car touring the wonderful state of Minnesota, my hope is that you have as much fun using this Activity Book as I did writing it.

Enjoy your Minnesota Experience—it's the trip of a lifetime!!

Carole Marsh

Geographic Tools

Beside each geographic need listed, put the initials of the tool that can best help you!

(CR) Compass Rose   (LL) Longitude and Latitude
(M) Map   (G) Grid
(K) Map key/legend

1. _____ I need to find the geographic location of Germany.

2. _____ I need to learn where an airport is located near St. Paul.

3. _____ I need to find which way is north.

4. _____ I need to chart a route from Minnesota to California.

5. _____ I need to find a small town on a map.

Match the items on the left with the items on the right.

1. Grid system

2. Compass rose

3. Longitude and latitude

4. Two of Minnesota's borders

5. Symbols on a map

A. Map key or legend

B. North Dakota and Iowa

C. A system of letters and numbers

D. Imaginary lines around the earth

E. Shows N, S, E, and W

ANSWERS: 1-LL; 2-K; 3-CR; 4-M; 5-G; 1-C; 2-E; 3-D; 4-B; 5-A

Minnesota's Magnificent Mineral

Minnesota has been the leading producer of iron ore in the United States since the opening of its iron ranges in the northeastern part of the state in the 1880s. The three major iron ranges are the Vermilion, Mesabi, and Cuyuna. Iron ore is shipped from the mines by railroad to ports on Lake Superior, where it is loaded onto special ships for transport to steel mills. Other leading products of Minnesota include sand, gravel and stone

Answer the following questions using the information above.

Minnesota leads the nation in the production of what important mineral?

_____

Name one of Minnesota's three major iron ranges.

_____

After the iron is mined, where is it shipped?

_____

What are Minnesota's three other leading mineral products?

_____

When did Minnesota first start producing iron?

_____

ANSWERS: 1-iron ore; 2-Mesabi, Vermilion, or Cuyuna; 3-ports on Lake Superior; 4-sand, gravel, and stone; 5-1880s

Minnesota Government

Minnesota's state government, just like our national government, is made up of three branches. Each branch has a certain job to do. Each branch also has some power over the other branches. We call this system checks and balances. The three branches work together to make our government work smoothly.

The executive branch enforces the laws. It includes a governor, lieutenant governor, secretary of state and attorney general.	The legislative branch makes and repeals the laws. It is made up of the Senate and House of Representatives.	The court judicial system includes the state court system which interprets the laws. It includes the state supreme court with a chief justice and six associate justices.
Executive Branch	**Legislative Branch**	**Judicial Branch**

For each of these government officials, circle whether he or she is part of the EXECUTIVE, the LEGISLATIVE, or the JUDICIAL branch.

1. the governor — EXECUTIVE LEGISLATIVE JUDICIAL
2. a local district representative — EXECUTIVE LEGISLATIVE JUDICIAL
3. a senator — EXECUTIVE LEGISLATIVE JUDICIAL
4. lieutenant governor — EXECUTIVE LEGISLATIVE JUDICIAL
5. the chief justice of the Supreme Court — EXECUTIVE LEGISLATIVE JUDICIAL
6. the speaker of the House of Representatives — EXECUTIVE LEGISLATIVE JUDICIAL
7. treasurer — EXECUTIVE LEGISLATIVE JUDICIAL
8. a district attorney — EXECUTIVE LEGISLATIVE JUDICIAL
9. a district court judge — EXECUTIVE LEGISLATIVE JUDICIAL
10. a member of the general assembly — EXECUTIVE LEGISLATIVE JUDICIAL

The number of legislators may change after each census.

ANSWERS: 1-executive; 2-legislative; 3-legislative; 4-executive; 5-judicial; 6-legislative; 7-executive; 8-judicial; 9-judicial; 10-legislative

All Around Minnesota! Bubblegram

Fill in the bubblegram by using the clues below.

1. Minnesota's state capital

2. Minnesota's largest city

3. City where buildings are made of Sioux quartzite

4. Childhood home of author Laura Ingalls Wilder

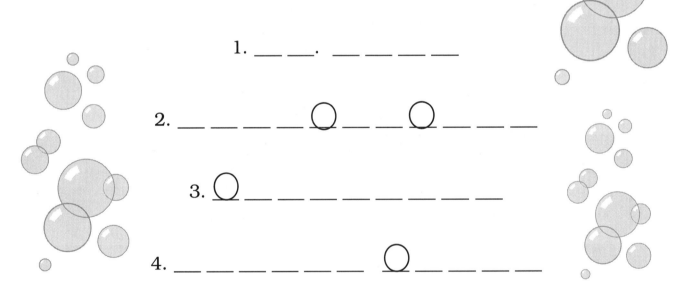

1. __ __. __ __ __ __ __

2. __ __ __ __ Ⓞ __ __ Ⓞ __ __ __

3. Ⓞ __ __ __ __ __ __ __ __

4. __ __ __ __ __ __ Ⓞ __ __ __

Now unscramble the "bubble" letters to find out the mystery words!

Hint: A familiar Minnesota animal and one of the state's nicknames!

The __ __ __ H __ R State!

Furs and Timber

Minnesota's rich supply of furs attracted many French-Canadian trappers and traders. Woodsmen called *voyageurs* paddled down Minnesota's rivers and hiked through thick forests to trade their packs of goods for fur pelts. The furs, especially beaver skins, were popular in England, where top hats made of beaver skin were all the rage. Grand Portage was the main fur-trading town in Minnesota.

Lumbering in Minnesota began in the 1830s. Logs were cut in the forests and floated down the rivers to mills, where they were trimmed into planks. Lumberjacks were numerous throughout the state and soon the famous legend of lumberjack Paul Bunyan was born.

The paragraphs below contain word puzzles called a rebus. Discover what words you need to fill in the blanks by looking at the picture clues. Sometimes it helps to say words aloud.

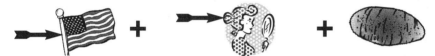

I am a popular character in a Minnesota folk legend about lumbering.

_____ _____

Minnesota's key fur trading town was called

_____ _____.

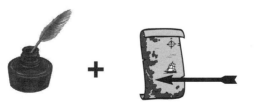

Name of the country where beaver pelts and hats were popular.

_____ _____.

ANSWERS: 1-Paul Bunyan; 2-Grand Portage; 3-England

Minnesota Wheel of Fortune, Indian Style!

The names of Minnesota's many Native American tribes contain enough consonants to play . . . Wheel of Fortune!

See if you can figure out the Wheel of Fortune-style puzzles below! "Vanna" has given you some of the consonants in each word.

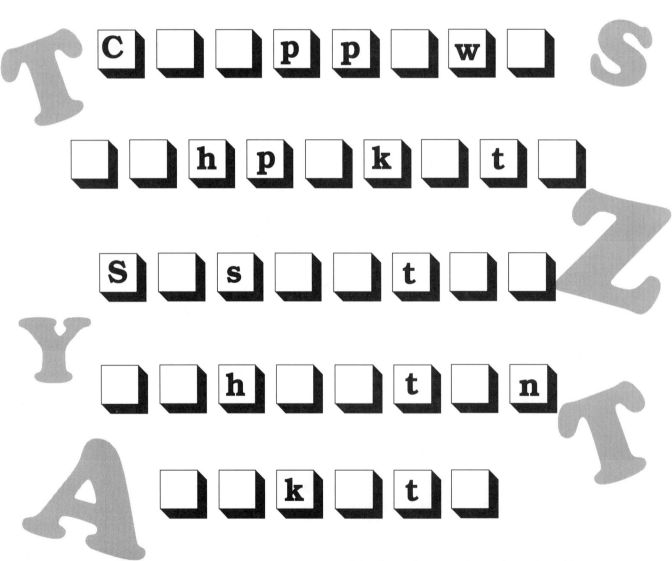

Rainbow, Pretty Rainbow

Rainbows often appear over Lake Superior after a storm. Rainbows are formed when sunlight bends through raindrops. Big raindrops produce the brightest, most beautiful rainbows. You can see rainbows early or late on a rainy day when the sun is behind you.

Color the rainbow in the order the colors are listed below, starting at the top of the rainbow. Then, in each band write down as many Minnesota-related words as you can think of that begin with the same first letter as that color!

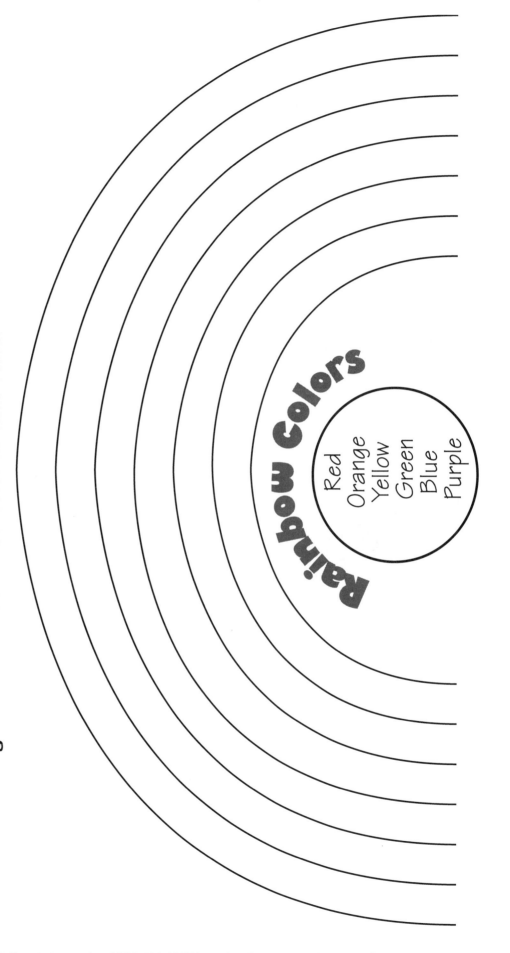

Rainbow Colors

Red
Orange
Yellow
Green
Blue
Purple

In the Beginning... Came a Colony

French fur traders first claimed Minnesota when they were searching for an all-water route to the Pacific Ocean. Although they never discovered a water route, French explorers and traders claimed much of the land in Minnesota for France.

Help the French fur traders find their way to Minnesota!

Zebulon Pike was sent to find suitable sites for forts after the Louisiana Purchase in 1803.

Minnesota

Finish

Start

FAST FACTS
- Jonathan Carver, an explorer from the East, wrote about his travels in Minnesota.
- Father Louis Hennepin, a Belgian missionary, was kidnapped by the Dakota in 1680.

U.S. Time Zones

Would you believe that the contiguous United States is divided into four time zones? It is! Because of the rotation of the earth, the sun appears to travel from east to west. Whenever the sun is directly overhead, we call that time noon. When it is noon in Minneapolis the sun has a long way to go before it is directly over San Francisco, California. When it is 12:00 p.m. (noon) in Brainerd, it is 12 p.m. (noon) in Chicago, Illinois. There is a one-hour time difference between each zone!

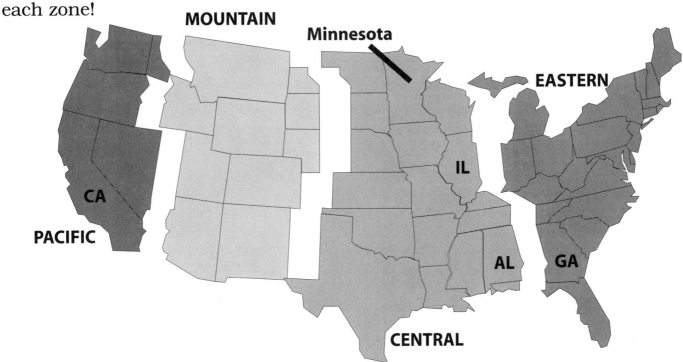

Look at the time zones on the map below then answer the following questions:

1. When it is 10:00 a.m. in Duluth, Minnesota, what time is it in California? _____ a.m.

2. When it is 3:30 p.m. in Atlanta, Georgia, what time is it in Minnesota? _____ p.m.

3. In what time zone is Minnesota located? _____

4. In what time zone is Colorado located? _____

5. If it is 10:00 p.m. in Sauk Centre, Minnesota, what time is it in Alabama? _____ p.m.

ANSWERS: 1-8:00 a.m.; 2-2:30 p.m.; 3-Central; 4-Mountain; 5-10:00 p.m.

Sing Like a Minnesota Bird Word Jumble

Arrange the jumbled letters in the proper order for the names of birds found in Minnesota.

Wild Turkey

Kingfisher

Bald Eagle

Warbler

Common Loon

Wood Duck

Mallard

Brown Thrasher

1. R W A B E L R _ _ _ _ _ _ _

2. G F I R E H S K N I _ _ _ _ _ _ _ _ _ _

3. L A L D M A R _ _ _ _ _ _ _

4. L B D A G A E E L _ _ _ _ _ _ _ _ _

5. O C M O M N O L O N _ _ _ _ _ _ _ _ _ _

6. R B W O N R H T H S A R E _ _ _ _ _ _ _ _ _ _ _ _ _

7. D O W O C U D K _ _ _ _ _ _ _ _

8. D L I W U T R Y E K _ _ _ _ _ _ _ _ _ _

Minnesota Schools Rule!

Education is a key priority among Minnesotans. Starting in the early 1820s, the first school opened at Fort St. Anthony. By 1849, lawmakers governing the territory passed a law to establish schools. Today, there are 62 public and 44 private colleges and universities. The University of Minnesota, founded in 1851, maintains its principal campus in the Twin Cities of Minneapolis and St. Paul. Some of the state's private colleges include the Minneapolis College of Art and Design; Carleton; St. Catherine's; St. Olaf; and Concordia College.

Complete the names of these Minnesota schools. Use the Word Bank to help you. Then, use the answers to solve the code at the bottom.

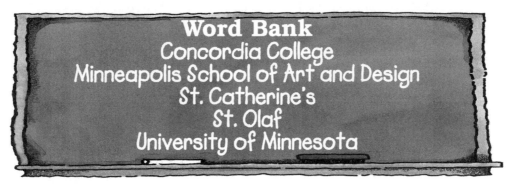

Word Bank
Concordia College
Minneapolis School of Art and Design
St. Catherine's
St. Olaf
University of Minnesota

1. University of __ __ __ __ __ __ __ __ __
                6 2

2. Minneapolis School of __ __ __ and __ __ __ __ __ __ __

3. St. __ __ __ __
          4

4. __ __ __ __ __ __ __ __ __ College
      5   1

5. St. __ __ __ __ __ __ __ __ __ __ ' __
          7

The coded message tells you what all college students want!

$$\frac{\quad}{1} \ \frac{\quad}{2} \ \frac{P}{3} \ \frac{\quad}{4} \ \frac{\quad}{5} \ \frac{\quad}{6} \ \frac{\quad}{7}$$

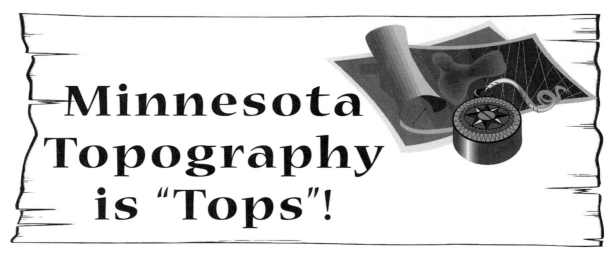

Minnesota Topography is "Tops"!

When we learn about Minnesota's topography, we use special words to describe it. These words describe the things that make each part of the state interesting.

Cross out every other letter below beginning with the first one to find out what each topographical term is!

1. P L T A S K J E: a body of water that is surrounded by land

2. H G Y L X A E C P I W E H R: a huge mass of ice that moves slowly over the land

3. T R O I B V W E M R: a large natural stream of flowing water

4. E S P U E P H E I R Y I Z O K R   Y U H P A L C A B N E D X S: a large stretch of hard rock in the northern part of the state

5. Y D O R M I W F Y T B L A E D S X S   D A T R O E Q A: a hilly region that borders Iowa and the Mississippi River in the far southeastern corner of the state

6. K T L I P L G L : a mixture of sand, clay, pebble and gravel that is good for farming

ANSWERS: 1-lake; 2-glacier; 3-river; 4-Superior Uplands; 5-Driftless Area, 6-till

Oh! Say Can You See...
The Minnesota State Flag

Minnesota's current state flag was adopted in 1957. It features a version of the state seal on a background of royal blue. The three dates on the flag represent Minnesota's first settlement date (1819), the year of statehood (1858), and the year the original flag was adopted (1893).

Color the state flag.

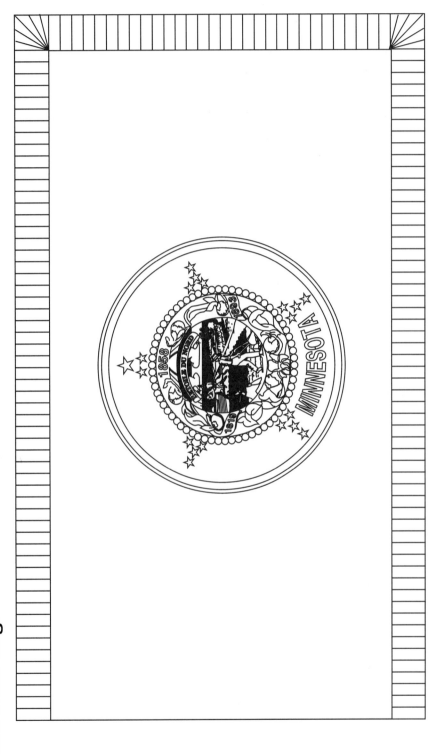

Design your own Diamante on Minnesota!

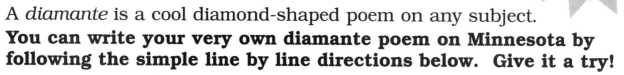

A *diamante* is a cool diamond-shaped poem on any subject.
You can write your very own diamante poem on Minnesota by following the simple line by line directions below. Give it a try!

Line 1: Write the name of your state.

Line 2: Write the name of the capital.

Line 3: Write the name of the state gem.

Line 4: Write a four-word state nickname.

Line 5: Write the state motto (French).

Line 6: Write the name of the state song.

Line 7: Write the name of the state butterfly.

_____

_____ _____

_____ _____ _____

_____ _____ _____

_____ _____

_____ _____

_____

YOU'RE a poet!
Did you know it?

History Mystery Tour!

Minnesota is bursting at the seams with history! Here are just a few of the many historical sites that you might visit. **Try your hand at locating them on the map! Draw the symbol for each site on the Minnesota map below.**

 Grand Mound, west of International Falls, is the largest prehistoric mound in the upper Midwest.

 Jeffers Petroglyphs, near Bingham Lake, has 2,000 rock carvings dating back to BC 3000.

 Sibley Historic Site in St. Paul is a stone residence that served the state's first governor.

 Voyageurs National Park, east of International Falls, was established in 1975. It contains and preserves thousands of acres of forest and waterways once traveled by fur trappers.

 Itasca State Park, near Bemidji, is one of the oldest parks in the country, It contains the headwaters of the Mississippi River.

 The Charles A. Lindbergh House in Little Falls was the boyhood home of the famous aviator who made the first nonstop flight between Paris and New York.

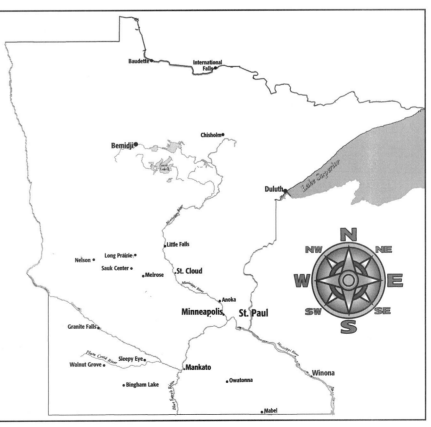

What in the World?

A hemisphere is one-half of a sphere (globe) created by the prime meridian or equator. Every place in the world is in two hemispheres (Northern or Southern and Eastern or Western). The equator is an imaginary line that runs around the world from left to right and divides the globe into the Northern Hemisphere and the Southern Hemisphere. The prime meridian is an imaginary line that runs around the world from top to bottom and divides the globe into the Eastern Hemisphere and Western Hemisphere.

Label the Northern and Southern Hemispheres.

Write E on the equator.

Is Minnesota in the NORTHERN or SOUTHERN Hemisphere? (circle one)

Color the map.

Label the Eastern and Western Hemispheres.

Write PM on the prime meridian.

Is Minnesota in the EASTERN or WESTERN Hemisphere? (circle one)

Color the map.

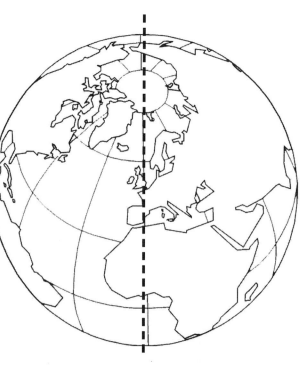

ANSWERS: Northern; Western

Places to go! Things to do!

Minnesota has so many cool places to go and so many cool things to do!
Use the Word Bank to help you complete the sentences below and learn about some of the exciting Minnesota sites you can visit!

1. _____ _____, near Fairfax, contains exhibits on the Dakota War and the history of settlement in the Minnesota Valley.

2. _____ features pipestone quarries and tall grass prairies covering 283 acres (115 hectares).

3. The _____ _____ _____ in Minneapolis includes an art museum, sculpture garden, and theater.

4. Learn about Minnesota's animals and nature at the _____ _____ Environmental Learning Center, near Finland.

5. The story of lumberjacking is told at the _____ _____ _____ in Grand Rapids.

6. Go stargazing at the Minneapolis Public Library and _____.

7. _____ National Forest, near Bemidji, covers 1.6 million acres (647,520 hectares) of big pine country.

8. The _____ Museum in Duluth tells the story of Minnesota's iron-rich history through exhibits.

WORD BANK

Wolf Ridge	Chippewa
Fort Ridgely	Depot
Pipestone	Planetarium
Walker Art Center	Forest History Center

ANSWERS: 1-Fort Ridgely; 2-Pipestone; 3-Walker Art Center; 4-Wolf Ridge Environmental Learning Center; 5-Forest History Center; 6-Planetarium; 7-Chippewa; 8-Depot

Please Come to Minnesota!

You have a friend who lives in Georgia. She is thinking of moving to Minnesota because she wants to be a home economist. Minnesota is a good place for her to work because of the many canned and frozen food plants in operation.

Write her a letter describing Minnesota and some of the home economist opportunities available.

_____
_____
_____
_____
_____
_____
_____
_____
_____
_____
_____
_____
_____
_____
_____
_____
_____
_____
_____
_____
_____
_____

Home economists also work for the Minnesota Department of Agriculture and at farm extension offices across state. They provide useful information to consumers and business people.

Criss-Cross Minnesota

Across

1. Site of the Twin Ports
2. Means "Blue Earth"
3. Site of pink quartzite quarry

Down

1. An Indian tribe native to Minnesota
2. Site of first permanent white settlement in Minnesota
3. Site of aviator Charles Lindbergh's boyhood home

Minnesota Rules!

Use the code to complete the sentences.

A	B	C	D	E	F	G	H	I	J	K	L	M	N	O	P
1	2	3	4	5	6	7	8	9	10	11	12	13	14	15	16

Q	R	S	T	U	V	W	X	Y	Z
17	18	19	20	21	22	23	24	25	26

1. State rules are called L A W S .
   12 1 23 19

2. Laws are made in our state C A P I T O L .
   3 1 16 9 20 15 12

3. The leader of our state is the __ __ __ __ __ __ __ __ .
   7 15 22 5 18 14 15 18

4. We live in the state of __ __ __ __ __ __ __ __ __ .
   13 9 14 14 5 19 15 20 1

5. The capital of our state is __ __ . __ __ __ __ .
   19 20   16 1 21 12

M I N N E S O T A ! ! !

Buzzing Around Minnesota!

Write the answers to the questions below. To get to the beehive, follow a path through the maze.

1. The capital of Minnesota is_ __. _ _ _ _ _ .
2. The largest prehistoric mound in the upper Midwest is
   _ _ _ _ _ _ _ _ _ _ _ _.
3. _ _ _ _ _ _ _ _ _ _ _ _ _ _ _ _ _ State Park contains a mosquito-infested swamp dreaded by early explorers.
4. An unusual boardwalk over a native bog can be found in _ _ _ _ _ _ _ _ _ _ _ _ State Park.
5. The _ _ _ _ _ _ _ _. _ _ _ _ _ _ _ farm near Elk River is a living history farm with costumed guides.
6. The _ _ _ _ _ _ _ _ _. _ _ _ _ House in Rochester is a mansion with a five-story entrance tower!
7. _ _ _ _ _ _ _ _ _ _ _ _ _ _ Wilder's Dugout is located near Walnut Creek.
8. _ _ _ _ _ _ _ _ _ _ _ _ _ _ in Minneapolis was the finest fort in the northwestern wilderness.
9. The University of _ _ _ _ _ _ _ _ _ _ _ in the Twin Cities has the largest library in the state.
10. St. John's _ _ _ _ _ _ _ _ _ _ _ _ _ in St. Cloud is part of St. John's University.

St. Paul

Savanna Portage

Start here

Grand Mound

Lake Bemidji

Minnesota

Abbey Church

Fort Snelling

Laura Ingalls

Oliver H. Kelley

William J. Mayo

ANSWERS: 1-St. Paul; 2-Grand Mound; 3-Savanna Portage; 4-Lake Bemidji; 5-Oliver H. Kelley; 6-William J. Mayo; 7-Laura Ingalls; 8-Fort Snelling; 9-Minnesota; 10-Abbey Church

Minnesota Through the Years!

Many great things have happened in Minnesota throughout its history. Chronicle the following important Minnesota events by solving math problems to find out the years in which they happened.

1. French traders become first known white men to visit Minnesota

   $9-8=$ $3 \times 2=$ $9-4=$ $3 \times 3=$

2. Britain takes Minnesota from France after the French and Indian War

   $10-9=$ $4+3=$ $10-4=$ $3 \times 1=$

3. Minnesota joins the Union as the 32nd state

   $10-9=$ $4 \times 2=$ $10-5=$ $18-10=$

4. Mayo family found the clinic in Rochester that bears their name

   $20-19=$ $16-8=$ $5+3=$ $3 \times 3=$

5. Present state capitol is completed

   $8-7=$ $15-6=$ $5 \times 0=$ $5 \times 1=$

6. Minnesotan Charles Lindbergh, Jr. makes nonstop trans-Atlantic flight

   $18-17=$ $4+5=$ $10-8=$ $4+3=$

7. Congress creates Voyageurs National Park

   $25-24=$ $11-2=$ $10-3=$ $6 \times 0=$

8. Presidential candidate Jimmy Carter selects Minnesotan Walter Mondale as his running mate

   $18-17=$ $17-8=$ $11-4=$ $11-5=$

9. Mall of America opens

   $15-14=$ $6+3=$ $13-4=$ $2 \times 1=$

10. Former professional wrestler Jesse Ventura elected governor

    $21-20=$ $3 \times 3=$ $12-3=$ $15-6=$

ANSWERS: 1-1659; 2-1763; 3-1858; 4-1889; 5-1905; 6-1927; 7-1970; 8-1976; 9-1992; 10-1999

What Did We Do Before Money?

In early Minnesota, there were no banks. However, people still wanted to barter, trade, or otherwise "purchase" goods from each other. Wampum, made of shells, bone, or stones, was often swapped for goods. Indians, especially, used wampum for "money." In the barter system, people swapped goods or services.

Later, banks came into existence, and people began to use money to buy goods. However, they also still bartered when they had no money to spend.

Place a star in the box below the systems used today.

Rhymin' Riddles

Minnesota Celebrities

1. I'm a musical artist with names to spare:
   I live in the Twin Cities, my fame I do share
   With young up-and-comers, who like to sing;
   "Paisley Park," "Purple Rain"; know the answer?

   Give a ring! My name is _____.

2. I'm known as a folk singer; the 60s were my decade;
   I grew up in Hibbing; my songs chronicled the tirade.
   Tunes about trains and rains and wind,
   I still write songs about where I've been.

   My name is _____.

3. Turn on public radio to hear my voice;
   I talk about Minnesota as my state of choice.
   Lake Wobegon is a special place;
   It serves as the setting for my show of good taste!

   My name is _____.

ANSWERS: 1-Prince; 2-Bob Dylan; 3-Garrison Keillor

Historical Minnesota Women World Wonders!

Minnesota has been the home of many brave and influential women. See if you can match these women with their accomplishments.

Eugenie Anderson
Patty Berg
Harriet Bishop
Elizabeth, Sister Kenny

Judy Garland
Judith Guest
Martha Ripley
Laura Ingalls Wilder

1. _____ teacher; came to St. Paul in 1849 from New England

2. _____ professional golfer who helped start the LPGA

3. _____ actress who starred as Dorothy in the *Wizard of Oz*

4. _____ writer and best-selling author of *Ordinary People*

5. _____ author of the Little House children's book series

6. _____ doctor and founder of Maternity Hospital

7. _____ nurse who developed a method for rehabilitating polio patients

8. _____ politician and first woman to serve as a U.S. ambassador

ANSWERS: 1-Harriet Bishop; 2-Patty Berg; 3-Judy Garland; 4-Judith Guest; 5-Laura Ingalls Wilder; 6-Martha Ripley; 7-Elizabeth, Sister Kenny; 8-Eugenie Anderson

Producers and Consumers

Producers (sellers) make goods or provide services. Ralph, a fourth grade student in Ely, is a consumer because he wants to buy a new wheel for his bicycle. Other products and services from Minnesota that consumers can buy include books, magazines, food processing and manufacturing of products such as electronics and medical equipment.

Complete these sentences.

Without cellophane tape, I couldn't

_____

_____

Without my computer, I couldn't

_____

_____

Without books and magazine, I couldn't

_____

_____

Without scientific instruments, I couldn't

_____

_____

Minnesota Word Wheel!

Use the Word Wheel of Minnesota names to complete the sentences below.

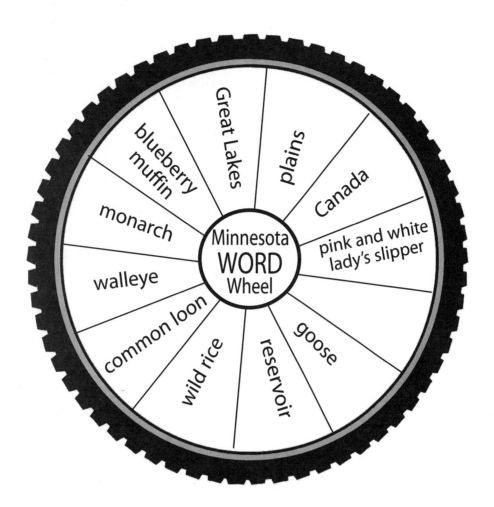

1. The state bird of Minnesota is the _____.

2. The state tree is the _____.

3. The state flower is the _____.

4. The state butterfly is the _____.

5. The state grain is _____.

6. The state fish is the _____.

7. Minnesota is a _____ _____ state.

8. The country that borders Minnesota is _____.

Minnesota's Mississippi

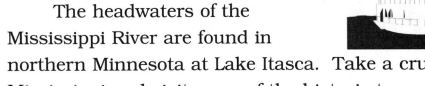
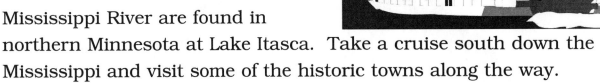

The headwaters of the Mississippi River are found in northern Minnesota at Lake Itasca. Take a cruise south down the Mississippi and visit some of the historic towns along the way.

Find the city along the Mississippi River, and fill in its name using the word bank below.

Word Bank

Brainerd   Little Falls   Minneapolis

St. Paul   Winona

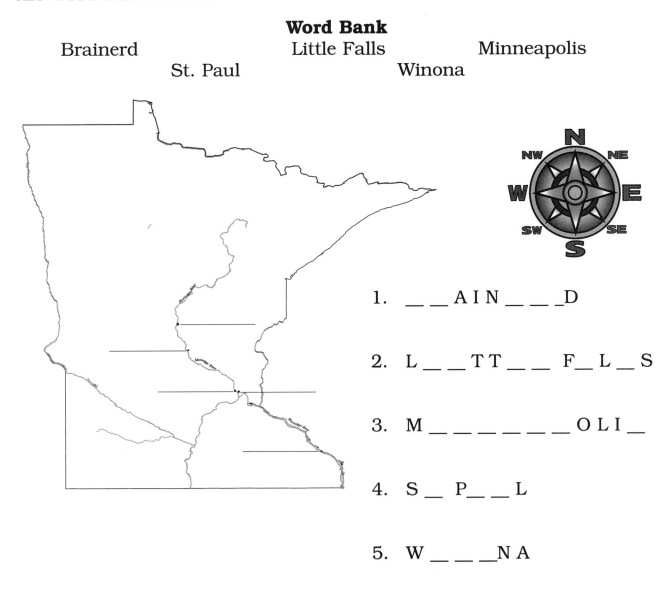

1. _ _ A I N _ _ _ D

2. L _ _ T T _ _ F _ L _ S

3. M _ _ _ _ _ _ _ O L I _

4. S _ P _ _ L

5. W _ _ _ N A

Create Your Own Minnesota State Quarter!

Look at the change in your pocket. You might notice that one of the coins has changed. The United States is minting new quarters, one for each of the 50 states. Each quarter has a design on it that says something special about one particular state. The Minnesota quarter will be in cash registers and piggy banks everywhere after it's released in 2005.

What if you had designed the Minnesota quarter? Draw a picture of how you would like the Minnesota quarter to look. Make sure you include things that are special about Minnesota.

Minnesota Law Comes In Many Flavors!

For each of these people, write down the kind(s) of law used to decide whether their actions are legal or illegal.

1. Bank robber _____
2. Business person _____
3. State park ranger _____
4. Minnesotans _____
5. Doctor _____
6. Real estate agent _____
7. Corporate president _____
8. Ship owner _____
9. Diplomat _____
10. Soldier _____

Medical Law

International Law

Military Law

Commercial Law

Maritime Law

Antitrust Law

Environmental Law

Property Law

Criminal Law

State Law

Mixed-Up States!

Color, cut out, and paste each of Minnesota's neighbors which include four states and two Canadian provinces onto the map below. Be sure and match the state shapes!

My friends are all mixed up! See if you can help them find their way back home!

MN

ON

IO

ND

WI

SD

MB

Minnesota—
Land of 10,000 Lakes

Minnesota is known for its picturesque lakes and waterways. One of the state's nicknames is the Land of 10,000 Lakes, but there are more than 15,000 small lakes on record! Lake Superior, which covers 2,546 square miles (6,594 square kilometers), forms the eastern border of northern Minnesota, and river systems including the Mississippi provide resources for boaters and fishermen. The Boundary Waters Canoe Area Wilderness links 2,000 lakes in the state by rivers, creeks, and portages. One in every six Minnesotans owns a boat.

When you're on board any kind of boat, you have to use special terms to talk about directions. Label the ship below with these terms:

bow: front of the ship
stern: back of the ship
fore: towards the bow
aft: towards the stern
port: left as you face the bow
starboard: right as you face the bow

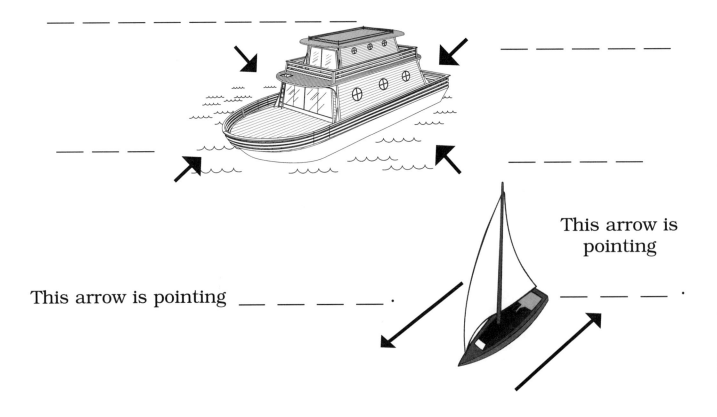

This arrow is pointing __ __ __ __ .

This arrow is pointing

__ __ __ __ .

Minnesota Politics As Usual!

On the lines provided, write down a question for each of the answers below. A hint follows each answer.

     Our elected government officials decide how much money is going to be spent on schools, roads, public parks, and libraries. Every election is important, and everyone who is eligible (able) to vote should do so!

     Today, many elected government officials are women. However, before the 19th Amendment to the U.S. Constitution, women were unable to vote in national elections! During World War I, Minnesota's women went to work in the factories while the men served overseas in the military. When the war was over, many women resisted returning to their traditional roles as homemakers. In 1920, enough states ratified the 19th Amendment, and it became the law of the land. Women gained total suffrage nationally, and continue to be a major force in the election process today.

1. Question: _____

    Answer: A draft of a law presented for review.

    (Short for William!)

2. Question: _____

    Answer: The right to vote.

    (Don't make us suffer!)

3. Question: _____

    Answer: The ability to forbid a bill or law from being passed.

    (Just say no!)

4. Question: _____

    Answer: The fundamental law of the United States that was framed in 1787 and put into effect in 1789.

    (Minnesota has one too!)

5. Question: _____

    Answer: An amendment.

    (It's not something subtracted from #4!)

ANSWERS: (may vary slightly) 1-What is a bill? 2-What is suffrage? 3-What is a veto? 4-What is the Constitution? 5-What is an addition to the Constitution called?

What Shall I Be When I Grow Up?

Here are just a few of the jobs that kept early Minnesotans busy.

Lawyer	Carpenter	Baker
Tenant Farmer	Weaver	Pharmacist
Woodcarver	Barber	Gaoler (jailer)
Judge	Gardener	Fisherman
Housekeeper	Mantuamaker (dressmaker)	Doctor
Silversmith	Printer	Governor
Politician	Cook	Milliner (hatmaker)
Dairyman	Musician	Soldier
Wheelwright	Bookbinder	Hunter
Teacher	Laundress	Blacksmith
Servant	Jeweler	Sailor
Cabinetmaker	Innkeeper	Beekeeper
Mayor	Stablehand	Gunsmith
Plantation Owner	Tailor	Prospector

You are a young colonist trying to decide what you want to be when you grow up.

Choose a career and next to it write a description of what you think you would do each day as a:

Write your career choice here!

_____

_____

_____

Write your career choice here!

_____

_____

_____

Write your career choice here!

_____

_____

_____

Write your career choice here!

_____

_____

_____

Governor of Minnesota!

The governor is the leader of the state.

You've been assigned to write a biography of the governor of Minnesota.

Before you can start your book, you need to jot down some notes in your trusty computer. Fill in the necessary information in the spaces provided on the dossier!

GOVERNOR'S NAME:

_____

_____

Date of Birth: _____
Place of Birth: _____
Father: _____
Mother: _____
Siblings: _____

Spouse: _____
Children: _____

Pets: _____

Schools Attended: _____

Previous Occupation(s): _____

Likes: _____

Dislikes: _____

abc · APPLICATIONS · MENU · CALCULATOR · FIND · 123

The ORIGINAL Minnesota Natives!

Minnesota's earliest inhabitants evolved into Mound Builders around 500 BC. The modern Dakota (Minnesota Sioux) people were descendants of the Mound Builders. In the late 1600s, Ojibwa (Chippewa), people moved west into Minnesota because of pressure from settlers to the east. The Dakota and Ojibwa were in constant warfare for decades.

The seven largest reservations in the state are Ojibwa, while the four smallest are Dakota. The largest reservation is Leech Lake, with more than 5,700 residents. Today, at least 90 percent of Minnesota's Indian population is Ojibwa; most of the remainder are Dakota.

What kinds of things did Native Americans use in their everyday life? For each of the things shown, circle YES if Native Americans did use it, or NO if they didn't.

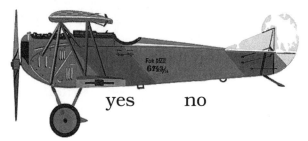

yes   no

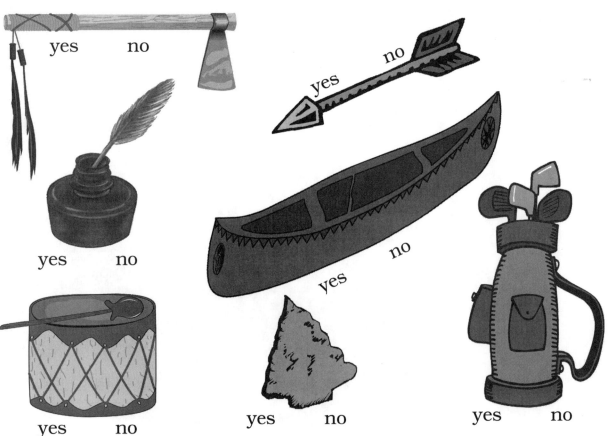

yes   no

yes   no

yes   no

no

yes

yes   no

yes   no

yes   no

States All Around Code-Buster!

Decipher the code and write in the names of the states and provinces that border Minnesota.

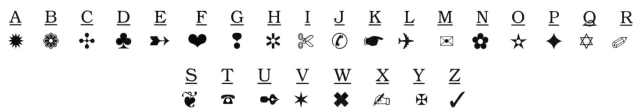

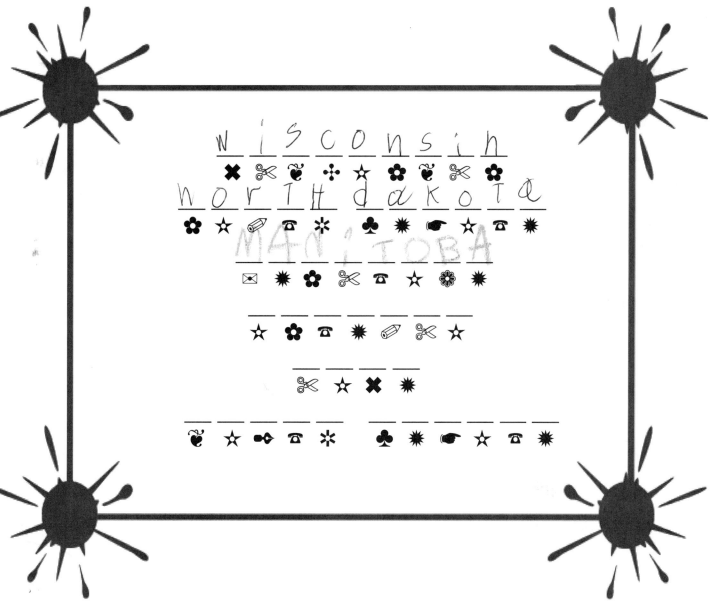

Unique Minnesota Place Names!

Can you figure out the compound words that make up the names of these Minnesota places?

Blueberry

Cherrygrove

Cottonwood

Finland

Goodridge

Holdingford

Maplewood

Northfield

Pipestone

Richfield

Shoreview

Springfield

Stillwater

Warroad

Wheaton

Looking For a Home in Minnesota!

Can you figure out where these things, people, and animals belong?

1. Laura Ingalls

   Bemidji

2. common loon

   Floating nest on Boundary Waters

3. record low temperatures

   Governor's Mansion

4. Jesse Ventura

   International Falls

5. Paul Bunyan and Babe

   Lake Wobegon

6. Garrison Keillor

   Minnehaha Falls

7. Hiawatha

   Target Center

8. Timberwolves

   Walnut Grove

ANSWERS: 1-Walnut Grove; 2-Floating nest on Boundary Waters; 3-International Falls; 4- Governor's Mansion; 5-Bemidji; 6-Lake Wobegon (It's a fictional home, of course!); 7-Minnehaha Falls; 8-Target Center (That's the Minnesota Timberwolves of the NBA!)

I Love Minnesota, Weather or Not!

Anyone who has ever watched the Weather Channel is familiar with International Falls, Minnesota. (And been glad they didn't live there during the frigid Minnesota winter!) The town of International Falls often records extremely low temperatures, often the nation's record low. Minnesotans are proud of their ability to handle cold and snow. The average winter temperature is only 8°F (-13°C). The lowest temperature ever was -60°F (-51°C) at Tower on February 2, 1996.

To put the Minnesota winters in perspective, a temperature or wind chill of around 30°F (-1.1°C) feels chilly and unpleasant. When the temperature or wind-chill drops between 0°F and –15°F (-17°C and – 27.2°C), it begins to feel very cold and very unpleasant. When the temperature reaches –20°F (-28.8°C), you may begin to get frostbite. When the temperature reaches -60°F (-51°C), the extreme cold makes all outdoor activity dangerous and frostbite likely. When the wind-chill drops below –60°F (-51°C), the frigid cold causes your exposed skin to freeze in less than 30 seconds! From December to February, the average low in International Falls is below zero, and the wind-chill makes it feel even colder!

But Minnesota can be steamy, too. The highest temperature recorded was 114°F (46°C) in Beardsley on July 29, 1917, and again in Moorhead on July 6, 1936.

On the thermometer gauges below, color the mercury red (°F) to show the hottest temperature ever recorded in Minnesota. Color the mercury blue (°F) to show the coldest temperature ever recorded in Minnesota.

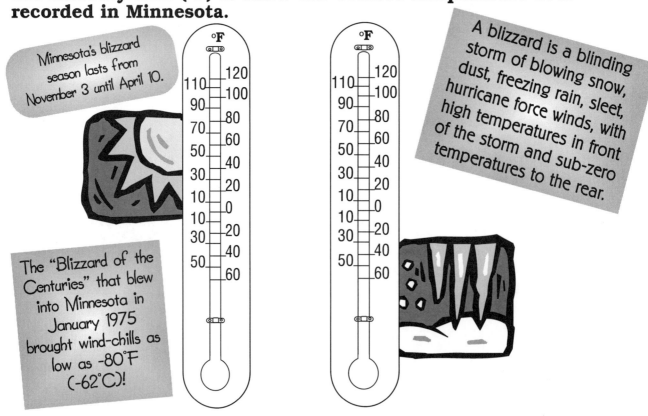

Minnesota's blizzard season lasts from November 3 until April 10.

The "Blizzard of the Centuries" that blew into Minnesota in January 1975 brought wind-chills as low as -80°F (-62°C)!

A blizzard is a blinding storm of blowing snow, dust, freezing rain, sleet, hurricane force winds, with high temperatures in front of the storm and sub-zero temperatures to the rear.

The Scenic Route

Imagine that you've planned an exciting exploratory expedition around Minnesota for your classmates. You've chosen some cities and other places to take your friends.

Circle these sites and cities on the map below, then number them in the order you would visit if you were traveling north to south through the state:

_____ Arches Museum of Pioneer Life, Winona

_____ Lake of the Woods County Museum, Baudette

_____ Lake Superior Museum of Transportation, Duluth

_____ Laura Ingalls Wilder Museum, Walnut Grove

_____ Minnesota Museum of Mining, Chisholm

_____ Science Museum of Minnesota, St. Paul

_____ Steam Engine Museum, Mabel

Key to a Map!

A map key, also called a map legend, shows symbols which represent different things on a map.

Match each word with a symbol for things found in the state of Minnesota.

airport
Minneapolis International Airport

church
Vasa Swedish Lutheran Church

mountains
Eagle Mountain

railroad
Burlington Northern

river
Mississippi River

road
I-94

school
Mankato State University

state capital
St. Paul

battle site
Fort Ridgely

bird sanctuary
Agassiz Wildlife Refuge

BROTHER, CAN YOU SPARE A DIME?

After the collapse of the stock market on Wall Street in 1929, the state of Minnesota, along with the rest of the nation, plunged headfirst into the Great Depression. It was the worst economic crisis America had ever known. Banks closed and businesses crashed...there was financial ruin everywhere.

Dwindling ore supplies had already threatened the mining industry in Minnesota. In the 1920s, there were 12,000 miners in Minnesota. During the Depression many were forced into work camps. By the 1930s there were only 2,000 miners left in the state. In the 1930s, Governor Floyd B. Olson was a strong supporter of President Franklin D. Roosevelt's New Deal and started a graduated state income tax and postponed farm foreclosures to help Minnesotans.

Our President Helps

While the nation was in the midst of the Depression, Franklin Delano Roosevelt became president. With America on the brink of economic devastation, the federal government stepped forward and hired unemployed people to build parks, bridges, and roads. With this help, and other government assistance, the country began to slowly, and painfully, pull out of the Great Depression. Within the first 100 days of his office, Roosevelt enacted a number of policies to help minimize the suffering of the nation's many unemployed workers. These programs were known as the NEW DEAL. The jobs helped families support themselves and improved the country's infrastructure.

Put an X next to the jobs that were part of Roosevelt's New Deal.

1. computer programmer _____

2. bridge builder _____

3. fashion model _____

4. park builder _____

5. interior designer _____

6. hospital builder _____

7. school builder _____

8. website designer _____

ANSWERS: 2 4 6 7

Minnesota Newcomers!

People have come to Minnesota from other states and many other countries on almost every continent! As time goes by, Minnesota's population grows more diverse. This means that people of different races and from different cultures and ethnic backgrounds have moved to Minnesota.

In the past, many immigrants have come to Minnesota from England, Sweden, Denmark, Germany, Norway, Finland, and many more countries! In the 1920s and 1930s, many African-Americans and Mexicans migrated to Minnesota. In the mid-1980s, many refugees came to Minnesota from Vietnam, Cambodia, and Laos. More recently, people from other parts of Asia and Pacific islands have immigrated to the state.

Read the statement and decide if it's a fact or an opinion. Write your answer on the line.

1. Many of Minnesota's early immigrants came from Europe.
   _____

2. Lots of immigrants speak a language other than English.
   _____

3. The clothing immigrants wear is very interesting.
   _____

4. Immigrants from Finland have a neat accent when they speak.
   _____

5. Many immigrants will become United States citizens.
   _____

6. People have immigrated to Minnesota from nearly every country in the world.
   _____

An immigrant is a person who migrates to another country in hopes of a better life.

ANSWERS: 1-fact; 2-fact; 3-opinion; 4-opinion; 5-fact; 6-fact

A Day in the Life of a Pioneer!

Pretend you are a pioneer in the days of early Minnesota. You keep a diary of what you do each day. Write in the "diary" what you might have done on a long, hot summer day in July 1869.

This Old House!

Take yourself back 100 years. Can you imagine what life would be like in the Victorian Era? What did turn-of-the-century Minnesotans own? How did they live?

See if you can pick out which of the following items people at the turn of the century had and which ones they did not.

Circle the things you might find or use around your 1900 home.

Home, Sweet Home!

Minnesota has been the home of many different authors. Here are just a few. See if you can locate their hometowns on the map of Minnesota below! Write the number of each author near the town where he or she lived.

1. Sinclair Lewis—novelist who wrote *Main Street,* the story of small town America, and *Babbit,* the tale of a man without standards; won the 1930 Nobel Prize for Literature. His home is south of Long Prairie between Melrose and Nelson.

2. F. Scott Fitzgerald—the storyteller of America's jazz age; best known for *This Side of Paradise* and *The Great Gatsby;* wrote *Tender is the Night* while living on Summit Avenue in Minnesota's capital city.

3. Maud Hart Lovelace—creator of the Betsy-Tacy series of books which tell the story from childhood to young adulthood of three young girls in Deep Valley, Minnesota. Deep Valley is based on her hometown, the big city between Sleepy Eye and Owatonna.

4. Laura Ingalls Wilder—the beloved author of the Little House series spent part of her childhood in Minnesota; she lived in a dugout house on the banks of Plum Creek. Her home was due south of Granite Falls and due west of Sleepy Eye.

5. Garrison Keillor—creator of *A Prairie Home Companion;* author of *Lake Wobegon Days* and *The Old Man Who Loved Cheese.* Head northeast from the Twin Cities, and you will come to his hometown before you get to St. Cloud.

ANSWERS: 1-Sauk Centre; 2-St. Paul; 3-Mankato; 4-Walnut Grove; 5-Anoka

Minnesota Spelling Bee!

**Good spelling is a good habit. Study the words on the
the page. Then fold the page in half and "take a spelling test" on
the right side. Have a buddy read the words aloud to you. When
finished, unfold the page and check your spelling. Keep your
score. GOOD LUCK.**

Each word is worth 5 points.

A perfect score is 100! How many did you get right?

agate

canoe

Chisholm

Dakota

Duluth

gopher

Hiawatha

homestead

immigrant

lumberjack

Minnehaha

Minnesota

Ojibwa

portage

prairie

Superior

taconite

Vikings

voyageur

walleye

Naturally Minnesota!

Fill in the bubblegram with some Minnesota crops and natural resources. Use the letter clues to help you.

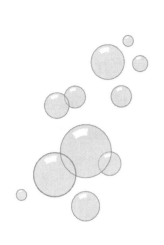
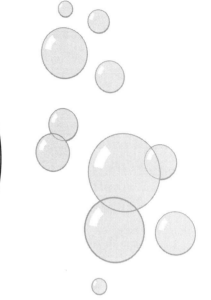

WORD BANK
blue catfish
iron ore
gravel
peat
shale
silica sand
taconite
vegetables
walleye
white-tailed deer
wild rice

1. ◯ h _ l _

2. w _ _ _ _ - _ _ l _ _ _ ◯ _ r

3. p _ _ ◯

4. _ _ _ _ d ◯ _ c _

5. t _ _ _ ◯◯ _ t

6. _ ◯ l l _ _ _

7. b _ _ _ _ ◯ _ f _

8. g _ _ ◯ _ _ _

9. _ ◯ _ _ c _ _ _ ◯ d

10. _ _ r _ _ ◯ r _

Now unscramble the "bubble" letters to find out the mystery word!
HINT: What is one way we can help to save our environment?

_ _ _ _ _ _ _ _ _ _ _ _

MYSTERY WORD: conservation

ANSWERS: 1–shale; 2–white-tailed deer; 3–peat; 4–wild rice; 5–taconite; 6–walleye; 7–blue catfish; 8–gravel; 9–silica sand; 10–iron ore

Voyage of the Voyageur!

Bonjour! Welcome to the watery world of the *voyageur*! I am from the wilds of a world called *Kanata*. You will see from my dress, I am prepared for action. The rich supply of beaver furs brings me and other French Canadian trappers to your state. Join me on my journey!

Some *voyageurs* from Thunder Bay come down the Kaministiquia River to Lac la Croix; others come from Lake Superior to the Pigeon and Rainy rivers but have to use more than 36 portages. When they come to a place their *canot du nord* (canoe) cannot go, they hike through thick forests with heavy packs on their backs and boats over their heads, that's a portage. I take the easy way— through the Lake of the Woods to the wilderness on the southern side!

On our long journeys we eat patties made of dried meat and berries called pemmican and hardtack, which are saltless, dried biscuits. We even drink out of our *ceinture fléchée*, the sashes we wear that are coated in beeswax. We use them to keep warm at night, to support the canoe during a portage, and to serve as a drinking cup in an emergency!

Number these words from the story about the *voyageur* in the order they would appear in alphabetical order:

_____ 1. biscuits

_____ 2. emergencies

_____ 3. southern

_____ 4. beeswax

_____ 5. wilderness

_____ 6. journey

_____ 7. canoe

_____ 8. portage

_____ 9. action

_____10. watery

_____ 11. trappers

_____ 12. hardtack

_____ 13. pemmican

_____ 14. *ceinture fléchée*

_____ 15. *voyageur*

_____ 16. *bonjour*

_____ 17. sashes

_____ 18. beaver

_____ 19. Canadian

_____ 20. French

ANSWERS: 4; 9; 16; 3; 20; 12; 7; 14; 1; 19; 17; 11; 13; 8; 18; 5; 15; 2; 6; 10

What a Great Idea!

Minnesota inventors and scientists have developed many products that make our lives easier and safer. **See if you can fill in the blanks with the correct innovation!**

WORD BANK

open heart	Post-it Notes
Scotch	skyscraper
photosynthesis	refrigeration
Scotchgard	union suits

Melvin Calvin of St. Paul won the Nobel Prize for chemistry in 1961 for tracing the path of carbon dioxide through plants. He learned how they make their own food in a process called _____.

Minnesota Mining and Manufacturing (3M) was making sandpaper when the company saw a need for masking tape to paint two-tone cars. The tape they developed didn't adhere very well, so laboratory technician Richard Drew turned it in to what we know today as _____® tape. And this mistake turned 3M into one of the most successful companies in Minnesota!

Art Fry kept trying to find a way to keep the page markers from falling out of his hymnals. He remembered that a scientist at his company had developed an adhesive that held but could be removed, so he tried the glue on the backs of paper scraps. The company's marketing department wasn't sure the product would sell, but they gave away some samples and everyone loved them. Fry had invented 3M's _____®.

Minnesota winters certainly make the need for warm clothing necessary. Wool keeps people warm, but wool next to the skin is scratchy. George Munsing of Minneapolis developed a way to combine wool and silk to make wool underwear more comfortable to wear. In 1891, his company began manufacturing one-piece underwear called _____.

Finding ways to keep warm would spur the creative thoughts of Minnesota inventors, but would you believe that _____ was also invented here? Fred Jones formed the Thermo King corporation after finding a way to cool a truck for a friend who was trying to deliver fresh foods and found the ice he used melted in hot weather.

In 1952, the world's first _____ surgery was performed by Dr. C. Walton Lillehei who is known as the "Father of _____ Surgery." He also developed a disposable heart-lung machine and helped develop cardiac pacemakers.

Patsy O. Sherman was the first woman inducted into the Minnesota Inventors Congress. She invented something mothers everywhere have sprayed on sofas and chairs to keep pets and children from leaving behind nasty stains— _____ ® stain repellant.

In 1888 Minnesota architect and engineer LeRoy Buffington patented a design for a tall steel frame to support buildings. His design transformed the skylines of the cities around the world. He is known as the "Father of the _____."

ANSWERS: 1–photosynthesis; 2–Scotch®; 3–Post-it Notes®; 4–union suits 5–refrigeration; 6–open heart; 7–Scotchgard®; 8–skyscraper

Famous Minnesota People Scavenger Hunt!

Here is a list of some of the famous people associated with our state. **Go on a scavenger hunt to see if you can "capture" a fact about each one. Use an encyclopedia, almanac, or other resource you might need. Happy hunting!**

Ann Bancroft _____

Patty Berg _____

Harry Blackmun _____

Robert Bly _____

Bob Dylan _____

Wanda Gag _____

Judy Garland _____

J. Paul Getty _____

Hubert H. Humphrey _____

Elizabeth, Sister Kenny _____

Little Crow _____

Charles Lindbergh _____

Roger Maris _____

Walter Mondale _____

Gordon Parks _____

Zebulon Pike _____

Charles M. Schultz _____

DeWitt Wallace _____

August Wilson _____

Dave Winfield _____

From the shores of Gitchee Gumee

Use the words in the word bank to fill in the blanks in this Minnesota legend. Some may be used more than once.

A long time ago, by the shores of the great lake _____ a baby was born to a beautiful woman. His father was the _____ _____, Mudjekeewis. Just after the boy was born his father flew away and his mother died of a broken heart. The boy whose name was _____ was raised by his grandmother _____, the daughter of the Moon who had long ago fallen to _____.

Although _____ was very old she took very good care of _____ and taught him the secrets of the sky and _____ and all its creatures. In the winter she taught him about the northern lights and in the summer about the Milky Way. She taught him about the whispering pines and the lapping waters and to know why _____ was wonderful.

_____ explained to _____ that the _____ was the heaven of flowers where the place _____'s blossoms went when they were faded. She taught him to listen to the _____, and he could learn their languages. The birds became _____'s friends and soon all the _____ did. He called them his brothers and sisters and understood that all creatures share one _____.

ANSWERS: Gitchee Gumee; West Wind; Hiawatha; Nokomis; Earth; Nokomis; Hiawatha; Earth; Earth; Nokomis; Hiawatha; Nokomis; Earth; rainbow; Earth; animals; Hiawatha; Hiawatha; animals; Earth

Map of North America

This is a map of North America. Minnesota is one of the 50 states.

Color the state of Minnesota red.

Color the rest of the United States yellow. Alaska and Hawaii are part of the United States and should also be colored yellow.

Color Canada green. Color Mexico blue.

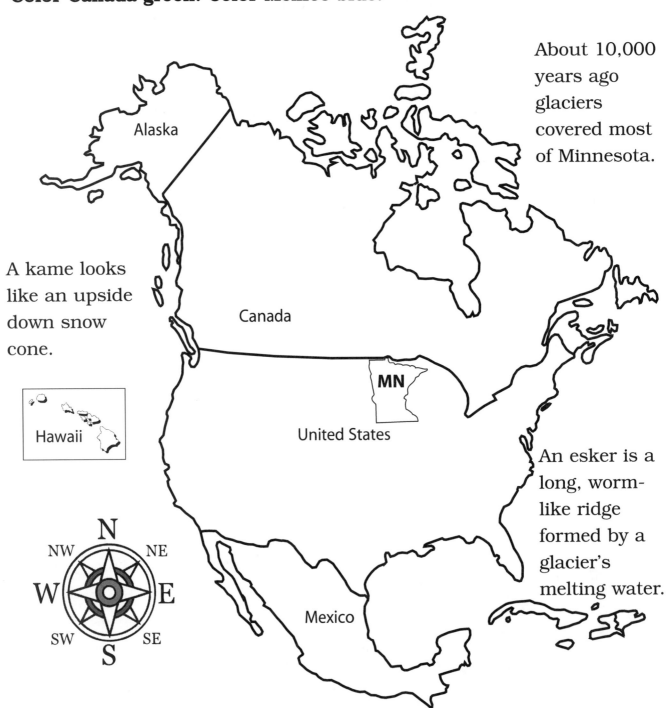

About 10,000 years ago glaciers covered most of Minnesota.

A kame looks like an upside down snow cone.

An esker is a long, worm-like ridge formed by a glacier's melting water.

Never Cry Wolf!

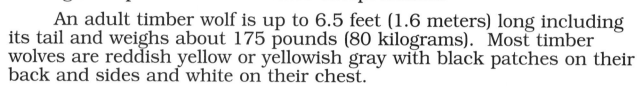

True
or
False?!

Timber, or gray, wolves *(Canis lupus)* are threatened in Minnesota. They once roamed all over Canada and the prairies of the Midwest. They are still abundant in northern Europe and Asia, but in North America, the timber wolf only lives in great numbers in Alaska and Canada. Smaller numbers exist in the Pacific Northwest and Minnesota. Under the Endangered Species Act, the timber wolf is listed as a threatened species in Minnesota and an endangered species in other states except Alaska.

An adult timber wolf is up to 6.5 feet (1.6 meters) long including its tail and weighs about 175 pounds (80 kilograms). Most timber wolves are reddish yellow or yellowish gray with black patches on their back and sides and white on their chest.

Wolves live on prairies, in forests, and on mountains. Individuals are carnivores who eat small animals and birds, but packs attack weak, old, or young caribou, reindeer, sheep, or other large mammals. Sometimes they eat carrion (the decaying flesh of dead animals). Since wolves are valuable predators in the food chain, their disappearance often leads to overpopulation of animals such as coyote and deer.

Many people believe wolves are dangerous to livestock, pets, and people. It's a myth that wolves attack people. They try to avoid contact with human beings. But the myths about wolves often hurt the attempts by biologists to re-introduce the species back into an area.

Read each sentence, and decide if it is TRUE or FALSE. Write your answers on the lines provided.

_____ 1. The timber wolf is another name for coyote.

_____ 2. Timber wolves are endangered in every state.

_____ 3. Timber wolves feed primarily on small animals and birds.

_____ 4. The timber wolf is dangerous to livestock, pets, and people.

_____ 5. Wildlife biologists have found it easy to re-introduce the wolf

into areas where the species is threatened.

ANSWERS: 1–false; 2–false; 3–false; 4–false; 5–false

Minnesota State Greats!

In the paragraph about important people from Minnesota below there are eight misspelled words. Circle the misspelled words, and then spell them correctly on the lines provided.

Minnesotans love thier sports! Form the early explorers racing canoes, birling, and climbing trees to the modern contests of Vikings, Lynx, Timberwolves, Twins, Wild, and Golden Gophers—the state has a rich tradition in sprots.

Minnesota Vikings quarterback Fran Tarkenton was inducted into the National Football Hall of Fame in 1986. He is the Vikings all-time leader in passing attempts, completions, yards, and touchdown passes. Five Twins have had their numbers retired Harmon Killebrew (number 3), Rod Carew (number 29), Tony Oliva (number 6), Kent Hrbek (number 14), and Kirby Puckett (number 34). The Twins one baseball's World Series in 1987 and 1991.

Timberwolves basketball all-stars have included Tom Gugliotta and Kevin Garnett. Forward Katie Smith is one of the Lynx stars. Ever year the University of Michigan and University of Minnesota football teams clash to win the Little Brown Jug. Bruce "Boo" Smith won the 1941 Heisman Trophy playing halfback for the Golden Gophers. He stared in a movie about his life called *Smith of Minnesota*. Another Minnesotan who gained fame in sports was Patty Berg. The golfer won 83 tournaments between 1935 and 1964. She helped found the Ladies Professional Golf Association (LPGA), and the LPGA named it's top award the Patty Berg Award.

Some of the state's greatest sports success has come in collegiate hockey; the Golden Gophers won the NCAA title in 1954, 1974, and 1979. Professional hockey returned to Minnesota in 2000 when the Minnesota Wild became and National Hockey League expansion team. The state had been without a pro hockey team since 1993 when the Minnesota North Stars left to become the Dallas Stars.

_____   _____

_____   _____

_____   _____

_____   _____

ANSWERS: their; from; sports; won; every; starred; its; an;
MATCHING: Lynx–Women's basketball; Timberwolves–Men's basketball; Twins–baseball; Vikings–football; Wild–hockey

Virtual Minnesota!

It's time to build your own website! We've given you pictures of things that have to do with Minnesota. Color and cut them out, and arrange them on a blank piece of paper to create a web page that will make people want to visit Minnesota!

Into the Great World with Betsy, Tacy and Tib!

Maud Hart was born in April 25, 1892, in Mankato, Minnesota. Like Betsy Ray in her famous series of children's books, Maud followed her mother around the house asking her to spell words for the books she had already begun to write by the age of five. The young writer would stash her stories—all written on lovely pink paper—in the trunk of an old maple tree which supposedly still stands in Mankato. When she was 10, a book of her poems was printed, and when she was 18, the *Los Angeles Times* bought one of her stories for $10.

After World War I, Maud married Delos W. Lovelace, a short story writer, and became Maud Hart Lovelace. Her first novel was published in 1926. When the couple's daughter Merian was born, Maud told her daughter stories about her Minnesota childhood and these stories gave the young author the idea for writing *Betsy-Tacy*. Readers loved the stories about Betsy Ray and her friend Anastasia, better known as "Tacy," Kelly. The early stories told about Betsy growing up in the small yellow cottage and Tacy moving into the rambling white house across Hill Street in Deep Valley, Minnesota. So Mrs. Lovelace took Betsy and Tacy and their friend Thelma, whom they called "Tib," through high school, college, into "the great world" and marriage.

"Of course, I could make it all up, but in these Betsy-Tacy stories, I love to work from real incidents," Maud wrote. She based her characters on her childhood friends and their experiences growing up in Mankato. Maud Hart Lovelace died on March 11, 1980. In the 1998 film *You've Got Mail*, the Storybook Lady, played by Meg Ryan, recommends *Betsy-Tacy* to one of her young customers. Mrs. Lovelace's books were introduced to a new generation of young readers.

Read each sentence, and decide if it is FACT or FICTION. Write your answers on the lines provided.

_____ 1. Maud Hart grew up in Mankato, Minnesota.

_____ 2. Betsy, Tacy, and Tib played on Hill Street in Deep Valley, Minnesota.

_____ 3. Maud Hart Lovelace created the characters Betsy and Tacy in bedtime stories for her daughter.

_____ 4. Tacy's real name was Anastasia Kelly.

_____ 5. *Betsy-Tacy* became popular again after it was mentioned in *You've Got Mail.*

ANSWERS: 1–fact; 2–fiction; 3–fact; 4–fiction; 5–fact

A River Runs Through It!

The state of Minnesota is blessed with many rivers. See if you can wade right in and figure out these rivers' names! **For each river code, circle every other letter (beginning with the second one) to discover the name!**

RIVER BANK	
Crow Wing	Rainy
Minnesota	Red River of the North
Mississippi	St. Croix

Circle every other letter to find the river's name.

1. This river certainly has a stately name!

   M N I E N T N O E T S D O S T T A

2. Save up for a trip to see this river one day.

   R P A Q I Z N E Y

3. M-I-crooked letter-crooked letter-I-crooked letter-crooked letter-I humpback-humpback-I is one way to spell this river's name.

   M S I P S M S J I S S M S S I P P P P M I

4. You won't find this river in the Virgin Islands but on the border separating Wisconsin and Minnesota.

   S G T X C P R A O U I Q X

5. Don't worry about taking flight on a canoe trip down the calm waters of this river.

   C S R P O A W M W V I L N M G

6. This colorful river has a name that tells where it is located *and* which way it flows!

   R P E F D G R P I L V X E S R P O C F E T Y H J E F N M O Q R K T Y H

Minnesota Firsts!

In 1966, Dr. Richard C. Lillehei and Dr. William Kelly performed the first pancreas transplant. In 1968, Dr. Robert Good performed the first bone marrow transplant. Then on October 3, 1977, the first mechanical heart valve was used at University of Minnesota.

In 1914, Greyhound Lines, the largest interstate passenger bus service in the country, got its start in Minnesota as "Bus Andy" when Andrew Anderson and Carl Wickman began carrying people between Hibbing and the mines in northern Minnesota in a large touring car.

In 1901, Alexander Anderson of Red Wing discovered how to puff air into rice grains. He sold the idea to a cereal company. It was popularized by Quaker Oats at the St. Louis World's Fair in 1904.

Tired of trying to get to their favorite winter sport locations on skis, Edgar and Allan Hetten and David Johnson built a machine with ski feet to transport them there. The first "iron dog" snowmobile was invented in 1954.

Five French Canadian Catholics built the state's first church in 1841. It was a 25-foot (7.6-meter) log cabin.

In 1980, two former high school hockey players from Minneapolis wanted to train during the summer, so they made a pair of roller skates with wheels in a line instead of a rectangle. They called their product Rollerblades.

The first school in Minnesota opened in the 1820s for children of officers and soldiers at Fort St. Anthony.

Which "first" happened first?

_____ First in-line skates
_____ First puffed rice cereal
_____ First snowmobile

ANSWER: First puffed rice cereal

Minnesota Gazetteer

A gazetteer is a list of places. For each of these famous Minnesota places, write down the town in which it's located, and one interesting fact about the place. You may have to use an encyclopedia, almanac, or other resource to find the information, so dig deep!

_____ 1. Steamboat Museum _____
_____

_____ 2. Jolly Green Giant _____
_____

_____ 3. Mall of America _____
_____

_____ 4. Mayo Clinic _____
_____

_____ 5. Metrodome _____
_____

_____ 6. Museum of Mining _____
_____

_____ 7. Tyrone Guthrie Repertory Theater _____
_____

_____ 8. United States Hockey Hall of Fame _____
_____

WORD BANK

Bloomington	Minneapolis
Blue Earth	Rochester
Chisholm	Winona
Eveleth	

A Pioneer Corn Husk Doll!

You can make a corn husk doll similar to the dolls Minnesota pioneer's children played with! Here's how:

You will need:
- corn husks (or strips of cloth)
- string
- scissors

1. **Select a long piece of corn husk and fold it in half. Tie a string about one inch (2.54 centimeters) down from the fold to make the doll's head.**

2. **Roll a husk and put it between the layers of the tied husk, next to the string. Tie another string around the longer husk, just below the rolled husk. Now your doll has arms! Tie short pieces of string at the ends of the rolled husk to make the doll's hands.**

3. **Make your doll's waist by tying another string around the longer husk.**

4. **If you want your doll to have legs, cut the longer husk up the middle. Tie the two halves at the bottom to make feet.**

5. **Add eyes and a nose to your doll with a marker. You could use corn silk for the doll's hair.**

Now you can make a whole family of dolls!

Minnesota Timeline!

A timeline is a list of important events and the year that they happened. You can use a timeline to understand more about history.

Read the timeline about Minnesota history, then see if you can answer the questions at the bottom.

1659   French traders become first known white men to visit Minnesota

1680   Father Louis Hennepin, a Belgian missionary, explores the upper Mississippi River Valley and is captured by Dakota Indians

1745   Ojibwa win battle with Dakota and drive them to southern and western Minnesota

1763   Britain takes Minnesota from France after the French and Indian War

1783   Treaty of Paris, ending the Revolutionary War, gives Eastern Minnesota to the United States

1797   David Thompson completes map of Minnesota area of Northwest Territory

1841   Father Lucian Galtier builds Catholic chapel that becomes center of present-day St. Paul

1884   First iron ore shipped from Minnesota

1889   Mayo family founds the clinic in Rochester

1927   Minnesotan Charles Lindbergh, Jr. becomes first person to make a solo, nonstop flight across Atlantic Ocean

1975   The Blizzard of the Centuries hits Minnesota January 9-12

1999   Former professional wrestler Jesse Ventura elected governor

Now put yourself back in the proper year if you were the following people.

1. A French priest builds a small church near your home in Pig's Eye and calls it St. Paul's. It must be _____.

2. Your parents don't believe a professional wrestler could ever get elected governor, but you tell them it will happen in _____.

3. You celebrate when you hear your hero has safely landed in Paris, making the first solo flight across the Atlantic in _____.

4. All the old timers remember the Great Blizzard and the Armistice Day Storm, but you know the storm the Blizzard of the Centuries took place in _____.

5. You are surprised to see the strange French traders coming near your home, the year must be _____.

6. You know that people will benefit from the medical breakthroughs that the Mayo Brothers will bring to Minnesota at their new clinic, the year must be _____.

ANSWERS: 1-1841; 2-1999; 3-1927; 4-1975; 5-1659; 6-1889

Minnesota State Economy!

Minnesota banks provide essential financial services.
Some of the services that banks provide include:
- They lend money to consumers to purchase goods and services such as houses, cars, and education.
- They lend money to producers who start new businesses.
- They issue credit cards.
- They provide savings accounts and pay interest to savers.
- They provide checking accounts.

Circle whether you would have more, less, or the same amount of money after each event.

1. You deposit your paycheck into your checking account. MORE   LESS   SAME

2. You put $1,000 in your savings account. MORE   LESS   SAME

3. You use your credit card to buy new school clothes. MORE   LESS   SAME

4. You borrow money from the bank to open a toy store. MORE   LESS   SAME

5. You write a check at the grocery store. MORE   LESS   SAME

6. You transfer money from checking to savings. MORE   LESS   SAME

ANSWERS: 1.more 2.more 3.less 4.more 5.less 6.same

I Am A Famous Person From Minnesota

From the Word Bank, find my name and fill in the blank.

WORD BANK

Daniel Emmett   Paul Manship

Judy Garland   LeRoy Neiman

Charles Lindbergh   Charles Schulz

1. I named my plane the *Spirit of St. Louis* and took off on Roosevelt Field on May 20, 1927, and landed a hero in Paris 33.5 hours later. My nickname was the Lone Eagle.
   Who am I? _____ _____

2. I was born in St. Paul and everyone called me "Sparky." I am famous for drawing an underachiever named Charlie Brown and a beagle named Snoopy.
   Who am I? _____ _____

3. I was born in St. Paul, too, and am most famous for my paintings of the Olympic Games. My wild color paintings hang in large space in buildings and ships all over the world.
   Who am I? _____ _____

4. I wrote the theme song of the Confederacy "Dixie," but I lived right here in St. Paul when I wrote it. My brother Lafayette was chief justice of the Minnesota Supreme Court.
   Who am I? _____ _____

5. You see my sculpture at Christmas when they show the lighting of the Christmas tree at Rockefeller Center in New York. I designed the Prometheus Fountain there and the gates at the Bronx Zoo.
   Who am I? _____ _____

6. I am best known as Dorothy in *The Wizard of Oz*. When I was growing up in Minnesota, everyone knew me as Frances Ethel Gumm or "Baby."
   Who am I? _____ _____

Mounds Abound in Minnesota!

Archaeologists have found the thousands of Indian mounds and village sites in Minnesota rich in relics. Minnesota's Native Americans lived in villages in open ground, rock shelters, and caves. The things they threw away near their doorways are our archaeological clues to the way they lived.

More than 10,000 earthen mounds have been identified in Minnesota. Early archaeologists Alfred J. Hill and Theodore Lewis located almost 8,000 before 1895. Most of the mounds are knobby hills, but some resemble birds, turtles, fish and other animals.

You are an archaeologist digging into a site near Grand Mound, the largest earthen mound in the Midwest. Below are pictures of some of the artifacts that you find. Now, you have to identify these strange objects and their uses. Write down what you think these things are for!

_____

_____

_____

_____

_____

_____

_____

_____

_____

_____

_____

_____

Minnesota Native Americans!

The Dakota, often called the Minnesota Sioux, were forest dwellers. Their food included wild rice and swamp roots. They wore deerskin shirts and leggings with fringes and embroidery. They rode horses, hunted with bows and arrows, and covered their dome-shaped wigwams with skins. Four major groups of the Dakota lived in central and northern Minnesota: the Mdewakanton, the Wahpekute, the Sisseton, and the Wahpeton.

The Yankton, the Teton, and the Cuthead were distant relatives of the Dakota. They roamed the western prairies near the Missouri River and lived in portable teepees so they could follow the buffalo.

The Ojibwa lived around Sault Ste. Marie, Michigan. Settlers pushed the tribe westward around the Great Lakes into Minnesota. The area around Lake Superior near what is now Duluth was their tribal ground. A band of Ojibwa, the Mukkundwa, known for pillaging camped near Leech Lake.

The Cheyenne, who were related to the Ojibwa, lived in southern Minnesota near the Blue Earth River. But by 1700 the Oto and Iowa who were cousins of the Dakota people occupied that area.

Draw a line from each group to its location on the map.

Dakota (Minnesota Sioux)

Yankton, Teton, Cuthead

Ojibwa

Cheyenne

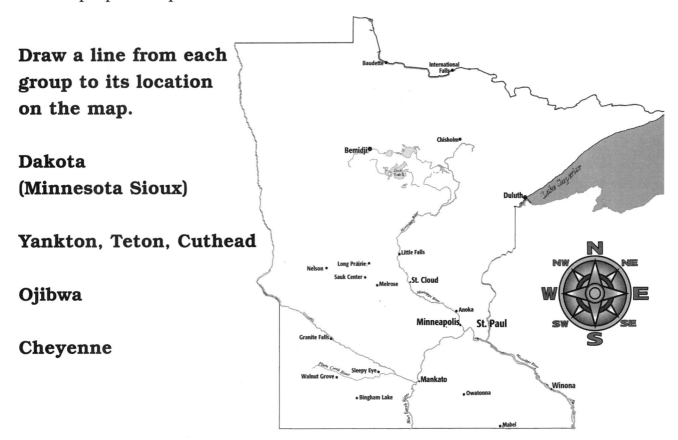

IT'S MONEY IN THE BANK!!

You spent the summer working at Dayton Hudson, and you made a lot of money...$500 to be exact!

Solve the math problems below.

TOTAL EARNED: $500.00

I will pay back my Mom this much for money I borrowed when I first started working. Thanks, Mom!

A. $20.00

subtract A from $500

B.   _3000_

I will give my little brother this much money for taking my phone messages while I was at work:

C. $10.00

subtract C from B

D.   _11.000_

I will spend this much on a special treat or reward for myself:

E. $25.00

subtract E from D

F.   _____

I will save this much for college:

G. $300.00

subtract G from F

H.   _____

I will put this much in my new savings account so I can buy school clothes:

I. $100.00

subtract I from H

J.   _____

TOTAL STILL AVAILABLE

(use answer J)   _____

TOTAL SPENT   (add A, C, and E)   _____

Minnesota's International Cities!

These cities may all sound like world capitals. But they can all be found right here in Minnesota—from Oslo in the northwest to Moscow in the southeast. Take a trip around the world without leaving Minnesota.

Circle the names of these cities, and you'll find the original name of St. Paul, which didn't sound like a world capital at all!

ALEXANDRIA	MONTEVIDEO	OSLO
CAMBRIDGE	MOSCOW	PADUA
FLORENCE	(NEW) MUNICH	(NEW) PRAGUE
GENEVA	NASSAU	SANTIAGO
(NEW) LONDON	NEW YORK (MILLS)	WARSAW
MILAN	ODESSA	

```
P  I  G  S  E  L  S  Y  E  S  X  A  G  B  P
A  U  A  J  Z  W  O  A  L  O  N  I  L  J  B
M  Q  Y  D  O  G  P  N  N  W  Z  R  Y  M  F
A  R  T  C  B  E  Q  R  D  T  U  D  Z  N  F
Y  X  S  F  O  N  Y  Y  A  O  I  N  F  E  C
A  O  Q  O  S  E  Z  Q  J  G  N  A  B  W  F
M  J  F  K  H  V  Y  O  C  C  U  X  G  Y  M
Z  K  R  R  L  A  D  A  D  B  I  E  Y  O  N
O  O  W  D  I  E  M  O  F  M  B  L  N  R  A
Y  W  L  A  S  B  Q  L  U  C  K  A  N  K  S
P  Y  H  S  R  E  C  N  E  R  O  L  F  N  S
Y  A  A  I  O  S  I  M  I  L  A  N  F  E  A
C  A  D  J  E  C  A  U  L  V  A  W  Q  W  U
F  G  B  U  H  E  O  W  A  A  L  T  D  I  D
E  B  Y  R  A  M  O  N  T  E  V  I  D  E  O
```

Geography Challenge: Try to locate these Minnesota cities' namesakes on a world map!

Numbering the Minnesotans!

STATE OF MINNESOTA
CENSUS REPORT

Every ten years, it's time for Minnesotans to stand up and be counted. Since 1790, the United States has conducted a census, or count, of each of its citizens. **Practice filling out a pretend census form.**

Name _____ Age [ ]

Place of Birth _____

Current Address _____

Does your family own or rent where you live? _____

How long have you lived in Minnesota? _____

How many people are in your family? _____

How many females? [ ] How many males? [ ]

What are their ages? _____

How many rooms are in your house? [ ]

How is your home heated? _____

How many cars does your family own? [ ]

How many telephones are in your home? [ ]

Is your home a farm? _____

Sounds pretty nosy, doesn't it? But a census is very important. The information is used for all kinds of purposes, including setting budgets, zoning land, determining how many schools to build, and much more. The census helps Minnesota leaders plan for the future needs of its citizens. Hey, that's you!!

Endangered and Threatened Minnesota!

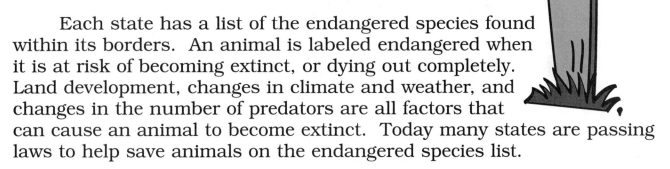

Each state has a list of the endangered species found within its borders. An animal is labeled endangered when it is at risk of becoming extinct, or dying out completely. Land development, changes in climate and weather, and changes in the number of predators are all factors that can cause an animal to become extinct. Today many states are passing laws to help save animals on the endangered species list.

Can you help rescue these endangered and threatened animals by filling in their names below?

1. B_ R _ _ W _ N _ _ W _

2. P_R _ _ _ I _ _ A _ _ _ N

3. _ _ I _ D' _ _ P _ R _ O _

4. F _ _ _-_ _ _ E _ S _ _ N _

5. _ A _ _ _ C _ E _ _ _ _ _ M _ S _ E _

Circle the animal that is extinct (not here anymore).

Hail, Minnesota: From the Gophers to the Capital!

In 1904 and 1905 two University of Minnesota students wrote a song for their alma mater (school attended). It was the official school song for 40 years until 1945 when it became the official state song. Only one phrase had to be changed. Instead of singing "Hail to thee our college dear" in the second line now we sing "Hail to thee our state so dear!"

"Hail! Minnesota"
By Truman E. Rickard
and Arthur E. Upson

Minnesota, hail to thee!
Hail to thee, our state so dear!
Thy light shall ever be
A beacon bright and clear.
Thy sons and daughters true
Will proclaim thee near and far.
They shall guard thy fame
And adore thy name;
Thou shalt be their Northern Star.

Like the stream that bends to sea,
Like the pine that seeks the blue,
Minnesota, still for thee,
Thy sons are strong and true.
From thy woods and waters fair,
From thy prairies waving far,
At thy call they throng,
With their shout and song,
Hailing thee their Northern Star.

Answer the following questions:

1. What two types of lights is Minnesota compared to in the song?

   _____

2. What three things will the sons and daughters of Minnesota do?

   _____

3. What are Minnesota's sons compared to?

   _____

4. What waves far in Minnesota, according to the song?

   _____

5. Where might your grandparents have heard this song before it became the official state song?

   _____

BONUS: What figures of speech are used in the song?

   _____

ANSWERS: (may vary slightly) 1 –beacon, star; 2– proclaim thee near and far, guard thy fame, and adore thy name; 3–stream and pine; 4–prairies; 5–at the University of Minnesota; Bonus: personification, metaphor, simile

Getting Ready To Vote in Minnesota

When you turn 18, you will be eligible to vote. Your vote counts! Many elections have been won by just a few votes. **The following is a form for your personal voting information. You will need to do some research to get all the answers!**

I will be eligible to vote on this date _____

I live in this Congressional District _____

I live in this State Senate District _____

I live in this State Representative District _____

I live in this Voting Precinct _____

The first local election I can vote in will be _____

The first state election I can vote in will be _____

The first national election I can vote in will be _____

The governor of our state is _____

One of my state senators is _____

One of my state representatives is _____

The local public office I would like to run for is _____

The state public office I would like to run for is _____

The federal public office I would like to run for is _____

Did you know that our state government has 67 senators?

The number of legislators may change after each census.

No, but I do know we have 134 representatives!

Minnesota State Seal

The official seal shows a barefoot farmer plowing a field near St. Anthony Falls on the Mississippi River. The farmer's axe, gun, and powder horn rest on a nearby stump. A Native American is riding a horse toward the farmer. In the background Norway pines are highlighted against a setting sun.

Color the state seal.

The Minnesota state seal has been revised three times, most recently in 1983.

Minnesota's state motto is *"L'Etoile du Nord,"* French for "star of the north." It also appears across the top of the seal.

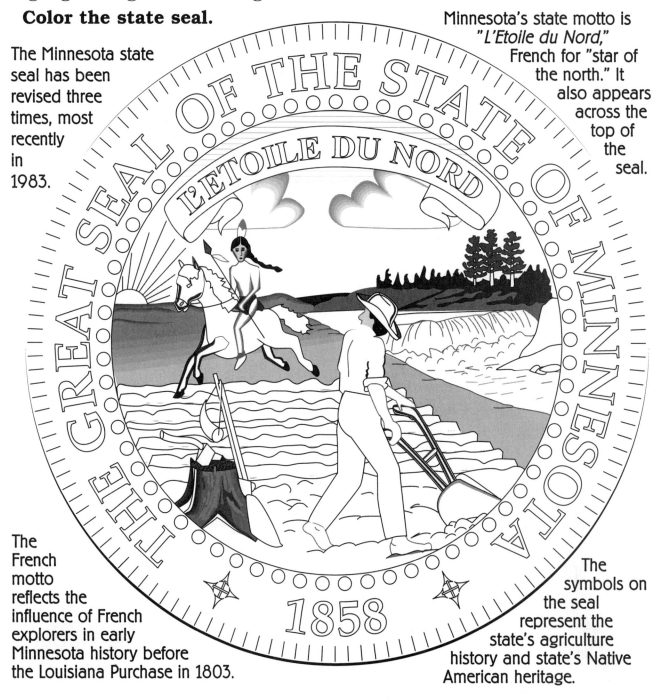

The French motto reflects the influence of French explorers in early Minnesota history before the Louisiana Purchase in 1803.

The symbols on the seal represent the state's agriculture history and state's Native American heritage.

Minnesota State Symbol Scramble!

**Unscramble the names of these symbols for the state of Minnesota.
Write the answers in the word wheel around the picture of
each symbol.**

1. N C O M O M   N O L O

   Hint: They live on floating nests in Boundary Waters.

2. N R A W O Y   I P E N

   Hint: This tree, like many Minnesotans, has Scandinavian roots.

3. L I D W   C I E R

   Hint: This grain was a Native American crop.

4. A H N M C R O   T U F T E B Y L R

   Hint: A regal name for this insect.

5. B B Y E R U R E L   N I M F U F

   Hint: I go well with the state beverage.

A Quilt Of Many Counties

Minnesota has 87 counties. The counties are governed by boards of commissioners who are elected.

– Label your county. Color it red.
– Label the counties that touch your county. Color them blue.
– Now color the rest of the counties green.

Contributions by Minnesota Minorities

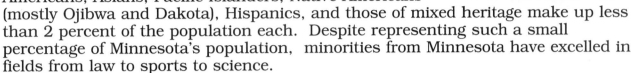

Although Minnesota has great cultural diversity, most of the population is descended from ethnic Europeans. Nearly 90 percent of the population is white. African-Americans, Asians, Pacific Islanders, Native Americans (mostly Ojibwa and Dakota), Hispanics, and those of mixed heritage make up less than 2 percent of the population each. Despite representing such a small percentage of Minnesota's population, minorities from Minnesota have excelled in fields from law to sports to science.

Frederick McGhee, a former slave, was the first African-American criminal lawyer west of the Mississippi River. He founded the Niagara Movement that later became the National Association for the Advancement for Colored People (NAACP). Alan Page began attending law school at the University of Minnesota while playing for the Minnesota Vikings. He was a part of the famous defensive line known as the "Purple People Eaters." After retiring from football, Page became a Minnesota Supreme Court Justice. He was inducted into the Pro Football Hall of Fame in 1988.

Japanese-American mechanical engineer Takuzo Tuschiya spent more than 40 years at General Mills. His inventions helped improve cereal protein processing and improved nutrition for people around the world.

Madonna Peltier Yawakie is president of TICOM, Inc, a telecommunications company in Brooklyn Park, Minnesota. She also serves as president of the Minnesota chapter of American Indian Science and Engineering and Science Society. The Society works to promote science and technical education among Native Americans and Alakasan natives so they will go into science and engineering careers. Ojibway artist Patrick Des Jarlait grew up on Red Lake Reservation but received little encouragement to paint. During World War II, he held a show of his paintings based on his childhood memories and each one sold.

Read each statement about these important Minnesotans and decide whether the statement is a FACT or an OPINION. Write your answer on the line.

1. Frederick McGhee was the first African-American criminal lawyer to practice west of the Mississippi River. _____

2. If Alan Page had not played for the Minnesota Vikings, he would not have become a Supreme Court Justice. _____

3. Without Takuzo Tsuchiya's innovations at General Mills, cereal would not taste as good. _____

4. Native Americans are not good at science._____

5. Patrick De Jarlait became an artist even though he was not encouraged to draw or paint as a child._____

ANSWERS: 1–fact; 2–opinion, 3–opinion; 4–opinion, 5–fact

Minnesota's Melting Pot

Minnesota is a melting pot of European **immigrant**. The great cultural diversity in the state leads to colorful and flavorful ethnic **diversity**. The **percentage** of foreign-born residents in Minnesota has been higher in Minnesota than in the rest of the United States. As late as 1930, the U.S. Census showed that more than half the population of the state had been born outside this country. The first Europeans to settle in Minnesota were French Canadians followed by Germans, Belgians, Scandinavians, Swiss, and Irish. In the 1900s, packing plants **recruited** workers from Balkan and Slavic countries so Romanians, Slovenians, Croatians, Poles, and Lithuanians began immigrating to Minnesota.

By the 1920s, European immigration slowed, but old world **customs** and folkways continued. You might still hear Czech spoken in New Prague, Polish in Winona, or Norwegian phrases creeping into talk all over Minnesota. It's not uncommon to have a *smorgasbord* at a Lutheran church social or to celebrate St. Lucia Day in a Swedish **community**. *Kolacky* is still prepared by Czech families with poppy seeds grown in their gardens

See if you can figure out the meanings of these words from the story above.

immigrant_____

_____

diversity_____

_____

percentage_____

_____

competition_____

_____

circulated_____

_____

recruited_____

_____

customs_____

_____

community_____

_____

Now check your answers in a dictionary. How close did you get to the real definitions?

Which Founding Person Am I?

From the Word Bank, find my name and fill in the blank.

? ? WORD BANK ? ?

Harriet Bishop   Zebulon Pike
Médard Chouart   Pierre Raddison
William Mayo   Henry Sibley
Alexander Ramsey

1. I was the first territorial governor of Minnesota and later served as governor and U.S. senator.

   Who am I? _____ _____

2. I was the first governor of Minnesota after it became a state.

   Who am I?_____ _____

3. I helped to organize the Minnesota territory and founded a hospital in Rochester. My sons accompanied me on medical rounds and became doctors who developed my hospital into a famous clinic.

   Who am I? _____ _____

3. I was the first white teacher in Minnesota. I came to St. Paul in 1849 from New England.

   Who am I? _____ _____

5. We were the first European explorers to reach Minnesota in 1654.

   Who are we? _____ _____ and

   _____ _____

6. After western Minnesota became part of the United States in the Louisiana Purchase in 1803, I made a treaty with the Dakota territories and established Fort Snelling. A mountain in Colorado is named after me.

   Who am I? _____ _____

ANSWERS: 1– Alexander Ramsey; 2–Henry Sibley; 3–William Mayo; 4–Harriet Bishop; 5–Pierre Raddison and Médard Chouart; 6–Zebulon Pike

!!It Could Happen— And It Did!

These historical events from Minnesota's past are all out of order. Can you put them back together in the correct order? Number these events from 1 to 10, beginning with the earliest. (There's a great big hint at the end of each sentence.)

_____Father Lucian Galtier builds Catholic chapel that becomes center of present-day St. Paul. (1841)

_____Minnesota joins the Union as the 32nd state. (1858)

_____Minnesotan Charles Lindbergh, Jr. becomes first person to make a solo, nonstop flight across Atlantic Ocean. (1927)

_____Vice President Hubert Humphrey, previous mayor of Minneapolis, loses a close presidential election to Richard Nixon. (1968)

_____Father Louis Hennepin, a Belgian missionary, explores the upper Mississippi River Valley and is captured by Dakota Indians. (1680)

_____Former professional wrestler Jesse Ventura elected governor. (1999)

_____Grain farmers and trade-union activists join to form Farmer-Labor Party. (1918)

_____Minnesota becomes one of the first states to form a department of conservation. (1931)

_____Women are granted the right to vote. (1919)

_____Four women are elected to Minnesota's state legislature. (1944)

ANSWERS in order they would appear: 2; 3; 6; 9; 1; 10; 4; 7; 5; 8

Canoe the Boundary Waters!

Northern Minnesota is home to the beautiful Boundary Waters Canoe Area Wilderness (BWCAW). Joining up with Quetico Provincial Park in Canada, the BWCAW includes nearly 2,000 lakes that are linked by rivers, creeks, and portages. These routes are available only to canoeists. When you take a trip through the Boundary Waters, you are living in the spirit of the *voyageurs*.

To navigate through the area, you must plan your trip carefully through lakes and rivers calculating your portage. During a portage you hoist your canoe over your head, support it on your neck and shoulders with the canoe yoke, and hike a trail to another waterway. The portages are measured in rods. A rod is 16.5 feet or 5.5 yards (5.02 meters). Canoe trips in the BWCAW are unlimited from easy courses to challenging ones. An easy route like Pine Creek Loop is a 22-mile paddle with four portages of 445 rods. A challenging route like Knife River-Disappointment Loop covers 34 miles and 18 portages of 1,377 rods.

Label the parts of this canoe and paddle. Use the Word Bank to help you.

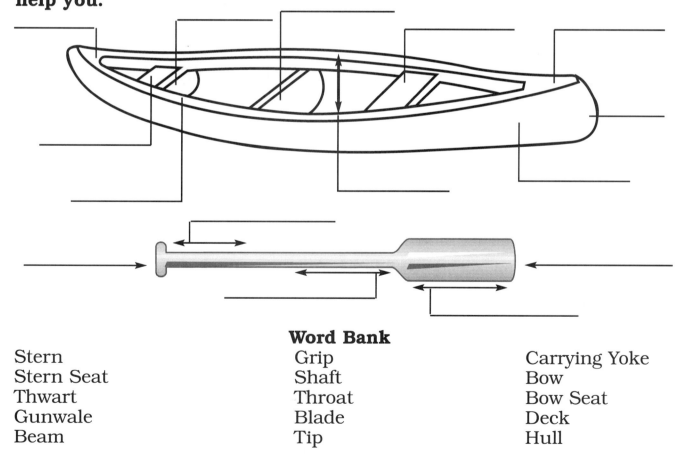

Word Bank

Stern	Grip	Carrying Yoke
Stern Seat	Shaft	Bow
Thwart	Throat	Bow Seat
Gunwale	Blade	Deck
Beam	Tip	Hull

Festivals, Fairs, and Fun!

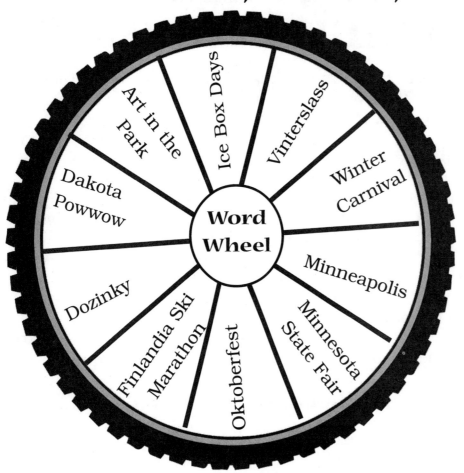

Using the Word Wheel of Minnesota names, complete the sentences below.

Word Wheel

Art in the Park · Ice Box Days · Vinterslass · Winter Carnival · Minneapolis · Minnesota State Fair · Oktoberfest · Finlandia Ski Marathon · Dozinky · Dakota Powwow

1. The _____ is a 12-day agricultural and educational exposition held on fairgrounds midway between St. Paul and Minneapolis.
2. _____ Festival is held every January in Grand Rapids.
3. In October you could go to _____to hear New Ulm's Concord Singers and eat lots of German food.
4. International Falls hosts _____, an annual winter festival held in January.
5. St. Paul's _____ is renowned for snow-sculpting competitions.
6. New Prague's Czechoslovakian Harvest Festival is called

   _____.
7. The Holidazzle Parade takes place in December in _____.
8. Avid skiers come out for the _____ each year.
9. Every September Mankato hosts the _____, a public meeting for a Native American tribe.
10. If you love art, you might want to see _____ held in July in Albert Lea.

ANSWERS: 1– Minnesota State Fair; 2–Vinterslass; 3–Oktoberfest; 4–Ice Box Days; 5–Winter Carnival; 6–Dozinky; 7–Minneapolis; 8–Finlandia Ski Marathon; 9–Dakota Powwow; 10–Art in the Park

Minnesota Pop Quiz!

Pop quiz! It's time to test your knowledge of Minnesota! Try to answer all of the questions before you look at the answers.

1. Minnesota's official nickname is:
   a) The Bread and Butter State
   b) The North Star State
   c) The Gopher State

2. The state flower of Minnesota is:
   a) prairie grass
   b) pink and white lady's slipper
   c) goldenrod

3. The state muffin and beverage are:
   a) blueberry and milk
   b) cinnamon and coffee
   c) bran and prune juice

4. The largest city in Minnesota is:
   a) St. Paul
   b) Duluth
   c) Minneapolis

5 The state motto *L'Etoile du Nord* is:
   a) Finnish
   b) French
   c) Norwegian

6. The state name comes from Dakota words which mean
   a) clear water
   b) cloudy water
   c) many water

7. The site of a major 18th century fur trading center in Minnesota is:
   a) Walnut Grove
   b) St. Croix
   c) Grand Portage

8. Which of these movies was filmed in Minnesota?
   a) *You've Got Mail*
   b) *The Mighty Ducks*
   c) *The X-Files*

9. Which of these things could you find in Minnesota?
   a) the world's largest ball of twine
   b) the world's largest bull statue
   c) the world's largest *smorgasbord*

10. The John Beargrease Sled Dog Race goes between
   a) Duluth and Grand Marais
   b) St. Paul and St. Cloud
   c) Winona and Thief River Falls

ANSWERS: 1-b; 2-b; 3-a; 4-c; 5-b; 6-b; 7-c; 8-b; 9-a; 10-a

The Gopher State!

Minnesota's official nickname is the North Star State, but it is often referred to as the Gopher State. Did you ever wonder how the state got that nickname? True gophers, or pocket gophers, are small, chubby animals that look like rats and burrow into the ground. Gophers ruin agricultural crops and destroy prairie grass and grain. It doesn't sound like a nice animal to have as a state mascot. But even the University of Minnesota is called the Golden Gophers.

The Minnesota gopher, which lives in most areas of the state, is actually a striped ground squirrel rather than a true gopher. It has 13 stripes alternating from light to dark. Their brownish and yellowish-gray color makes them look gold. Although they destroy crops, too, they are much cuter and look like chipmunks.

But the state didn't get the nickname from the animal. In early 1800s the state nickname was The Beaver State. In 1857, some lawmakers wanted to issue bonds to help the railroads expand. An editorial cartoon showed the legislators carrying bags of money, bribes from the railroad company. On their backs were train tracks and cars pulled by nine gophers. The gopher cartoon became famous, and Minnesota became known as "The Gopher State."

In 1927, Dr. Clarence Spears began calling his University of Minnesota team "the gophers" after the state animal. In the 1930s the press began calling the team the "golden swarm," and soon they became the Golden Gophers, a name now used by all University of Minnesota Twin Cities teams. Goldy, the gopher mascot, was a cute striped Minnesota gopher but now is a fierce pocket gopher. Fans must not care about the negative connections to gophers because they buy gopher teeth and wear them to Golden Gopher games!

In each pair of sentences below, one of the statements is false. Read them carefully and choose the sentence that is not true. Cross out the false sentence, and circle the true sentence.

1. Minnesota's official nickname was once the Beaver State.
   Today the official nickname is The Gopher State.
2. True gophers destroy agricultural crops.
   Minnesota gophers are actually ground squirrels that do not damage agricultural crops.
3. Minnesota gophers are gray and black and have 12 stripes.
   They look like cute chipmunks.
4. The Gopher State was adopted as the official nickname in 1857 by the legislature.
   An editorial cartoon that included gophers caused people to begin calling Minnesota "The Gopher State."
5. The University of Minnesota football team was sometimes called "the golden swarm."
   University alumni dislike the negative associations of with their school mascot.

ANSWERS: 1–The second sentence is false. 2–The second sentence is false. 3–The first sentence is false. 4–The first sentence is false. 5–The second sentence is false.

Paul Bunyan and Babe, the Blue Ox!

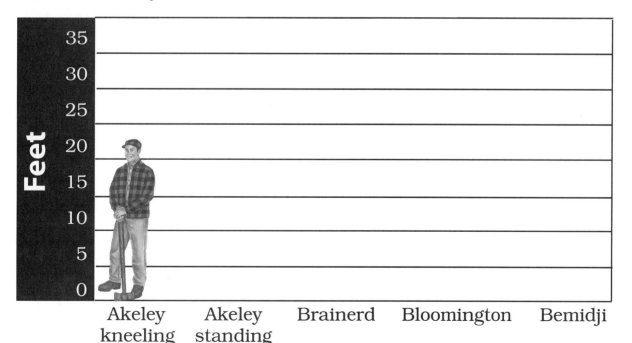

According to legend, Paul Bunyan was born in a forest near Brainerd in northern Minnesota. He was so big it took 17 storks to deliver him to his mother. He weighed 100 pounds (45.35 kilograms) when he was born. He always knew he wanted to be a lumberjack. He loved playing Pickup Sticks, grabbing trees out of the ground and tossing them in the air. His best friend was Babe, the Blue Ox. He rescued Babe from a block of ice in Pelican Lake. She had been frozen there since the Ice Age. Paul and Babe's footprints are what made Minnesota's 10,000 lakes.

Paul and Babe are so popular in Minnesota, there are nine statues in their honor. The tallest statue is 20 feet (6.096 meters) in Akeley, and this lumberjack is only kneeling. He would be 33 feet (10.05 meters) tall if he were standing! Brainerd, his birthplace, has a 26-foot (7.92-meter) tall talking statue. At the Mall of America in Bloomington, there is 19-foot (5.79-meter) tall statue of Paul and another statue of him in the Museum of Mining in Chisholm.

But the most famous statue is the one in Bemidji. Anyone who has visited Bemidji has probably had a photo taken with Paul Bunyan and Babe, the Blue Ox. The giant statues were built for a Paul Bunyan Carnival in 1937. Mayor Earl Bucklen was the model for Paul, but the statues are bigger than life-size. They are scaled 3:1. That means for each foot of human scale, the statue is three times as big. The statue of Paul is 18 feet (5.48 meters) tall. It took 737 man-hours to build. The statue is built on steel and concrete footings up to water level that weight 5.5 tons (4.95 metric tons). The statue frame is built of wood with reinforcing bars. Heavy steel laths cover the bars. Painted cement stucco covers the laths. The statue above the footings weighs 2.5 tons (2.25 metric tons) The statue of Babe weighs 5 tons (4.5 metric tons).

Graph the heights of the statues of Paul Bunyan in Minnesota. The first one has been done for you.

Laughing Water, Minnehaha Falls!

Minnehaha Creek runs into Minneapolis to a cataract creating Minnehaha Falls. The beautiful falls drop 53 feet (16 meters). The Falls have inspired generations of artists, composers, and poets.

In 1852, Alex Hesler made daguerreotypes (primitive photographs) of Minnehaha Falls. He gave one to a friend who was a neighbor of poet Henry Wadsworth Longfellow. Longfellow made Minnehaha Falls in famous in his poem "The Song of Hiawatha." Composer Anton Dvorak came to Minnesota to see the falls and composed "Opus 100, The Indian Maiden," supposedly on his shirtsleeve. Jacob Henrik Gerhard Fjelde's famous statue of Hiawatha and his beloved Minnehaha, whom he named after the Falls, stands near the Falls in the park today.

A *haiku* is a three-line poem with a certain number of syllables in each line.

Look at the example below:

> The first line has 5 syllables
> Min/ne/ha/ha Falls
>
> The second line has 7 syllables
> Laugh/ing wa/ter, last/ing love
>
> The third line has 5 syllables
> Hi/a/wa/tha calls

Now, write your own *haiku* about the amazing Minnehaha Falls!

_____

_____

_____

Shipwrecked!

Water and boats have always been an important part of Minnesota's history. From the *voyageurs* who first explored the northern waters in canoes to the lumber companies who shipped their logs on Lake Superior, the state's waterways have been important to the growth of the state. But shocking shipwrecks always occurred throughout shipping season on Lake Superior.

Ship	Date Wrecked	Type of Vessel	Location of Wreck	Cause of Wreck
George G. Hadley	June 7, 1902	288-foot wooden ship	just outside Duluth Ship Canal in Lake Superior	Collision with *Thomas Wilson*
Thomas Wilson	June 7, 1902	308-foot steel whaleback freighter	just outside Duluth Ship Canal in Lake Superior	Collision with *George G. Hadley*
Samuel P. Ely	October 30, 1896	200-foot three-masted wood schooner barge	Two Harbors	Broke lose from *Hesper's* tow in storm
Hesper	May 3, 1905	250-foot wood bulk cargo steam freighter	reef southwest of present day Silver Bay	Nor'easter tossed ship onto a reef

Answer the following questions based on the chart:

1. How many of the ships that sank were made of wood?

   _____

2. What two ships collided?

   _____

3. How many ships were wrecked because of storms?

   _____

4. Which of the ships that sank was the largest?

   _____

5. Which of the ships sank the earliest?

   _____

ANSWERS: 1–three; 2– George G. Hadley and Thomas Wilson; 3–two; 4–Thomas Wilson; 5–Samuel P. Ely

How Big is Minnesota?

Minnesota is the 12th largest state in the United States. It has an area of 86,943 square miles (225,182 square kilometers).

Can you answer the following questions?

1. How many states are there in the United States?

   _____

2. This many states are smaller than our state:

   _____

3. This many states are larger than our state:

   _____

4. One mile = 5,280 _____ _____ _____ _____

   HINT:

5. Draw a square foot.

6. Classroom Challenge: After you have drawn a square foot, measure the number of square feet in your classroom. Most floor tiles are square feet (12 inches by 12 inches). How many square feet are in your classroom? _____

   Bonus: Try to calculate how many classrooms would fit in the total area of your state. _____

   Hint: About 46,464 average classrooms would fit in just one square mile!

ANSWERS: 1-50; 2-10; 3-39; 4-feet; 5-answers will vary **Bonus:** 4,039,719,552 classrooms!

All the World's A Stage!

In 1959, Irish theater director Sir Tyrone Guthrie wanted to develop a new kind of theater in the United States. Most theater was in New York City—on Broadway–the great theater street in Manhattan. Guthrie and his partners decided that the Twin Cities was the perfect place to start a theater. It was in the heartland. It had a major university and many small colleges. And the city was enthusiastic about starting a theater.

The Guthrie Theater opened on May 7, 1963. Sir Tyrone directed William Shakespeare's *Hamlet*. The theater concentrated on producing great works of dramatic literature by Anton Chekov, Henrik Ibsen, Moliere and others. Guthrie also wanted to develop the artistic talent of actors, directors, designers who worked there. In 1982, the Guthrie Theater received a Tony Award for its outstanding contribution to the American theater.

Guthrie died in 1971. The theater's seventh artistic director is Joe Dowling, who worked at the Dublin's Abbey Theater. The Abbey is the National Theatre of Ireland.

A new Guthrie theater center is being built on banks of the Mississippi River. There will be three stages. Classic plays will be performed on a thrust theater like Shakespeare used. A proscenium stage will be used for 20th century plays. And a small studio theater will be used to develop new plays.

Answer these questions about The Guthrie Theater:

1. What country are the first and current artistic directors of The Guthrie Theater from? _____

2. Name some of the playwrights whose works are produced by The Guthrie Theater._____

_____

3. What kind of theater did Tyrone Guthrie want to develop?

_____

4. How many and what kind of stages will the new Guthrie theater complex have? _____

5. What award did The Guthrie Theater receive and why?

_____

ANSWERS: 1–Ireland; 2-answers may include Shakespeare, Moliere, Ibsen, Chekov and others; 3-a regional theater that focused on literature and development of artists; 4-three–thrust, proscenium, studio; 5-The Tony Award, for contributions to American theater

Minnesota Marches Into the Millennium!

The words below are known as an acrostic. See if you can make up your own acrostic poem describing Minnesota. For each letter in Minnesota's name, write down a word or phrase that describes Minnesota. The first is done for you.

M ade for high technology

I _____

N _____

N _____

E _____

S _____

O _____

T _____

A _____